Gardening
Under the Arch

*Homespun hints, recipes and money saving tips from the
rigorous high country of the chinook zone
by the Millarville Horticultural Club*

ISBN 0-88925-406-0

Published by
Millarville Horticultural Club
Box 76
Millarville, Alberta
Canada, T0L 1K0
(403) 931-3119
(403) 256-9100

First Printing, 1982
Second Printing, 1982
Third Printing, 1983
Fourth Printing, 1986
Fifth Printing, 1990 (Revised)
Sixth Printing, 1993

Printed and bound in Canada by
Friesen Printers
a Division of D.W. Friesen & Sons Ltd.
Ste. 120, 3016-19 Street N.E.
Calgary, Alberta
T2E 6Y9

Head Office
Altona, Manitoba R0G 0B0
Canada

Alpine clematis

Dedication

To all who garden in spite of
Jack Frost and Johnny Chinook

Acknowledgements

Compiling a book such as this has been an exercise in group co-operation. Our sincere thanks go to all members and friends who supplied articles, hints and information about so many aspects of gardening. We are grateful also to all who submitted their favorite recipes for the final section. We wish to thank all those who served on the book committee, typing, editing, revising, illustrating and checking material. From the many pictures submitted by members, a few of the best were chosen. We regret that there was not room for more.

For financial help we are most grateful to the following for grants:

New Horizons - for a generous grant for preparation of the book for printing.

Alberta Horticultural Association - for a generous grant toward printing.

The AHA also reviewed the book and made some helpful suggestions.

Foothills Municipal District #31 - for a grant toward printing.

Interest free loans have been received from the Millarville Racing and Agriculture Society and from the Millarville Recreation Board. For these we are indeed thankful.

To the Red Deer Lake School and the High River Office of Alberta Agriculture we are indebted for the extensive use of their photocopy machines and the hundreds of copies used to edit and proof read the material.

Millarville Horticultural Club

Table of Contents

Foreword

When first we embarked on this project there were just two of us with a goal in mind but a rather muddy vision of how best to achieve it. To start the project rolling, questionnaires dealing with general gardening matters were given to all the members of our club. Upon their return it quickly became clear to us that an editing committee would be required to review all the material submitted.

With great relief we found that those members we approached to sit on this committee were more than willing to help and indeed this attitude of willingness to help has been the reason behind the accomplishments of the Millarville Horticultural Club.

With the formation of this group of men and women of all ages and interests, the project slowly began to taxi down the runway. Meeting initially at each other's homes we began to discover how best to tackle our project and work effectively as a unit. Soon the project was in full flight with weekly meetings at which we had a delightful time developing the book's concept and content, all the while adding to our knowledge of gardening and of each other. It has been a happy experience.

Our aim has been to provide a book which we hope will be useful to all gardeners, whether they have been gardening for years or are just starting out. We share with you a love of gardening and all the special moments it brings; from the first sunny day in spring when you start to dig your beds, to that cold winter's day when you enjoy a fresh baked pie made from the fruit you have grown. We share too your pride in the sea of colour you have created with your flower beds; we watch with you all the beautiful birds flitting from shrub to vegetable patch; and we understand your tinge of sorrow as the autumn frost ends it all for another year.

That our book is now completed means our project is finished. That it is of help to you means it has been a success.

Sandi Gregg
Millarville Horticultural Club

Introduction

So, you live in the foothills of the chinook zone? Think of Maytime, and a crabapple in full bloom reels under the weight of wet snowfall. A bright July morning and you awaken to find marigolds, beans and potatoes blackened by a hard frost. Early December, and you hang Christmas lights in shirtsleeves while the smoke of a grass fire dims the horizon. Boom! Forty below, the power lines are singing, but the chickadees are silent, and you wonder why you didn't join your neighbour on a tropical holiday. Late February, and a lone butterfly dances above a brown lawn in a futile search for nectar.

Extremes and variation. No other words can adequately describe the climate of the foothills. A beautiful and scenic place to live, but with a climate so baffling that it is unlike anywhere else on Earth where gardening as we know it is practiced. A detailed section on climate alone has been added to throw light on some of these mysteries.

Yet despite the climatic extremes, one does find beautiful yards and bountiful gardens throughout the foothills chinook zone. It is no small miracle that man could settle this region and develop such a high level of horticultural expertise in so short a time.

Once hardy plants are well established in the gardens of this region, their care and demands are little different from any other gardening zone. Choosing the right things and getting them established is the great challenge and the key to success here. This is not the sort of place where one can plop a recommended plant into the ground, forget about it, then expect to gain encouraging results.

Hence, the book starts at the grass roots with a major section on garden management, the steps and methods which make all else possible. The various chapters and sub-sections are written by those living in this region; people who have mastered and refined their techniques through years of experience.

Wherever possible, time-saving or cost-saving tips have been recorded. One should never become a slave to one's garden. It is something to be enjoyed; and, that is the tone in which the information is presented.

Under various categories, there are thorough lists of the plants known to grow well in this region. Such lists represent almost a hundred years of trial and error. Looking down these lists, newcomers and oldtimers alike might be amazed at just how many wonderful things can be easily grown. As a long-time resident, Theresa Patterson, once said: "Enough nice things grow here; we needn't grieve for those that don't."

Those who are not satisfied to stick with only the tried and true are the ones who help such lists to grow as the years go by. Whether at an amateur or professional level, horticultural experimentation is a never-ending process. On the one hand, a person could fill an entire yard with the number of new introductions and hybrids that come out each year and appear worthy of trial. Or, one might be the first to succeed with an old favourite from some far away and completely different clime. For sure-fire results and to create the sound basis of an overall gardening strategy, use the lists and techniques in conjunction with each other. At the same time, do not be afraid to experiment, borrow and adapt from what is going on elsewhere.

Jon Lowry

Chapter One

Climate
and Weather

By Jon Lowry

In most gardening zones one can talk about the 'norm'; the normal growing season, the normal rainfall, the normal maximum and minimum temperatures. These norms are based on averages calculated from several decades of record keeping. Elsewhere, gardeners can plan and plant according to the norm because there is often little variation from year to year. In the high country of the chinook zone, *variation* is the norm.

It is interesting to note that in a newspaper article which listed 10 of the greatest weather extremes ever recorded in Canada, 5 of them have occurred in or very near our zone:

The greatest series of snowstorms occurred within a brief period of time from Claresholm south to the international border, where record snowfalls from 5-6½ feet of snow fell in two storms, a week apart, between April 17 to 20 and April 27 to 29, 1967.

The most rapid temperature change in one hour: 57 Fahrenheit degrees, from -20°F at midnight to plus 37°F at 1 a.m. on January 27, 1962 at Pincher Creek, needless to say during the onset of a very strong chinook.

Canada's lowest relative humidity was measured at Calgary at 3 pm, March 22, 1968, where it reached six per cent at the airport.

The greatest snowfall ever to occur in one day, 44 ins. was at Livingston Lookout Tower, in the Rocky Mountain foothills on June 29, 1963.

The worst hailstorm in Canada took place near Rocky Mountain House on July 11, 1970, where tennis ball-size hail fell.

On Facing Page
Top: May 19th, 1977. Note flowering crab at right.
Centre: End of August 1977.
Bottom: Hoar frost, a welcome sign of winter humidity.

1

Another article discussing winter temperatures, had this to say:

Last month's temperatures contrasted sharply with those of January, 1981. Last year, the Temperature never reached -4°F. We also recorded 10 days with maximum temperatures greater than 50°F, including Jan. 20, when the mercury reached 67°F, establishing a new record high for the month.

Winter Climate

The very thing which makes our area the most pleasant winter climate of anywhere between the Rockies and the Great Lakes is the one thing which most limits our choice of planting material: those warm, dry chinook winds. Most cold climate parts of the continent turn cold in fall and stay that way until spring thaw. The snow that falls, eventually builds up to insulate and protect plants, or at least their roots, from the coldest mid-winter temperatures. Snow also helps to keep the level of humidity relatively high, a condition which (nearly) all types of plants prefer.

Once or twice a decade our area does experience a truly snowy winter, and the evergreens always look that much fresher for it the following spring. Alas! This is not the norm. Statistically, December is our driest month, when three or four times in a decade we celebrate what is locally dubbed as a 'Brown Christmas', referring to the colour of the lawns.

And so, the trees, shrubs and ground covers that do best year upon year in the chinook zone must have a high degree of resistance to winter dessication. Without snow cover, the frost penetrates more deeply. A dry wind in winter robs plant moisture above ground, which the plant cannot replace if the root zone is almost thoroughly frozen. The foothills and higher elevations of the general chinook zone have the greatest limitations because the chinook blast is stronger and the cold spells colder than in adjacent zones to the east and north.

A great many landscaping books and gardening guides written for North America divide the continent into about 10 hardiness zones. Florida and southern California are assigned to zone 10, and the numbers decrease towards the coldest zone, zone 1, which lies adjacent to the Canadian Shield. The highest mountains are given a 2 and the Prairies and Great Plains are largely in zone 3. Correspondingly, all plant material recommended in such books is also assigned a number like 4, which says that the plant will not survive in any zone colder than 4, but will probably thrive in any zone that is warmer. Our zone is usually assigned to a boundary area between zone 3, the prairie and zone 2, the mountain areas.

To lump the chinook zone into such a method of hardiness classification can be very misleading. The system is based entirely upon average minimum winter temperatures. Hardiness in the chinook zone, and especially in the high country of the chinook zone is more a question of temperature *and* dryness. Our minimum winter temperatures are no more severe than other so-called zone 3 places like upstate New York, the Dakotas, or central Maine and New Brunswick. The books based on zone classification according to temperature only always suggest that we should be able to grow the things that thrive in such snowy, but equally cold areas: several types of oaks and maples, lindens, Russian olive, tea roses, columnar 'cedars', and so on. Such things growing in our zone are apt to be severely dwarfed or treated like annuals. We might be able to coax them along in an extremely sheltered part of the yard where there is snow build-up. But these are not the things which form the strong basis of a garden or shelter-belt planting. They will not adapt, or rather, they have not yet been hybridized to adapt to the winter dessication of chinook conditions.

Plants from other equally cold but wetter zones have another problem in trying to adapt. Those other zones are generally 2000 feet (700 meters) lower and hence experience a longer growing season. Plants from those places are on a different timeclock. They will leaf out too early for our zone and suffer severely if tender new growth is destroyed by a hard frost in late spring. Should they make it through spring unscathed, they will not go into dormancy soon enough for the first hard fall frost. The trees and shrubs which thrive here will have stopped growing by mid-August. The new growth should be hardened off and next year's buds well-formed by Labour Day. If not, a woody plant will suffer tip kill by the following spring.

One theory has it that we can successfully grow oaks, maples or lindens here by *not* over tending them. The idea is to put them in areas where they are growing in competition with other things. In other words, in a lawn or border, if the root zone is not cultivated and fertilized, such plants will leaf out later and harden off earlier. There seems to be merit to this approach when one sees places like Mary Dover's garden where a tree-form Amur maple is doing quite nicely in amongst native willows and grasses. The planting of such things is not an exercise for the impatient gardener. Most of them are very slow growing, and if we find ways to shorten their growing season so that they can survive, we slow them down even more. It can take decades for a Bur oak to gain enough substance to provide a noticeable addition to the garden. However, such things can live for centuries and to plant them is to provide for the enjoyment and instruction of future generations.

On this matter of growing zones, one should not completely reject any book which fails to make distinctions for the chinook climate. It is better to supplement your gardening library with locally written material which makes the proper distinctions. One of the best sources is a free Horticultural Guide published by Alberta Agriculture. It maps out the gardening zones with much greater accuracy and makes several distinctions between the varying degrees of rainfall, humidity and length of growing season. All plants listed under several basic categories are graded according to chinook hardiness; and the Guide is frequently updated to list the newest hybrids.

Chinook Winds

The Japan Current generates a great mass of warm, moist air which is continually hovering over the ocean several hundred miles west. If, when and where that air moves inland, at what speed and what altitude depends on the patterns of the winds and the positions of high and low pressure areas. In the depths of a winter cold snap, many foothills residents have learned to pay heed to reports of a low pressure system forming in the Gulf of Alaska. This is often the first sign that a chinook spell 'may' be only a day or two away. According to the weatherman, such a low pressure system in the right position will set off a counter-clockwise wind current which pushes the Pacific air eastward.

In winter, when that warm moist air first hits the cooler land mass along the coast, precipitation is the result. Rain or snow is heaviest wherever moist air is forced to rise against a wall of mountains. Relieved of its moisture, the drier air crosses a mountain range and becomes warmer as it loses altitude on the other side. If one drives from the West Coast towards our region, it is very apparent that the west or ocean-facing side of each successive mountain range is always more lush than the eastern slopes. Some of the interior valleys are so dried by the waves of warm falling air that they can be classed as semi-desert. This is evidenced by the sage and Ponderosa pine around Windermere, or the Kamloops/Okanogan area.

Moving eastward, the last and greatest ascent for the Pacific air currents is when they finally encounter the Rockies. If the air hasn't enough push to cross the continental divide we won't experience chinook conditions. However, if the westerlies are powerful enough to clear the Rockies at 15,000 feet or higher, the effect on this side is quite dramatic. Scientists have actually worked out a formula for how the air heats up on the eastward descent: an increase of 4½ degrees Fahrenheit for every 1000 foot drop in elevation. In other words, air dropping 10,000 feet will heat 45 degrees F by the time it hits ground level. As residents know, the thermometer can record such a temperature change in a matter of hours.

What makes the chinook phenomenon so baffling and unpredictable is that sometimes the warm air may not touch near ground level at all; nor will it necessarily even touch all parts of the zone evenly. And so, we have situations where two towns 19 miles apart have a significant temperature difference of 50 degrees Fahrenheit. In the Bow River Valley, the streets of downtown Calgary may be recording chilly, freezing temperatures while at the tops of the skyscrapers and in the higher towns and suburbs towards the foothills the temperature readings are downright balmy.

Summer Climate

While our relatively snow-free winters impose one set of limitations on what can be grown in this zone, summer has its own peculiarities. An extract from the diary of Betty Nelson, who gardens on a site about 25 miles southwest of Calgary at 4300 feet, gives a graphic first-hand description of the situation:

1970	Planted veg. garden 1st week May.	Good year, corn ready Aug. 12.	Fall frost Sept. 9
1971	Planted Veg. garden 1st week May.	Hard frost July 3.	Hard frost Sept. 14
1972	Planted veg. garden 1st week May.	Cold spring & summer.	Hard frost Sept. 20
1973	Planted veg. garden 1st week May.	Hot May. Frost June 10.	Hard frost Sept. 15.
1974	Planted veg. garden 1st week May.	Wet May, hot June.	Hard frost Sept. 1.
1975	Planted veg. garden 2nd week May.	Dry, late spring. Hail July 3.	Hard frost Sept. 3.
1976	Planted veg. garden 2nd week April.	1st half April hot & dry. Frost June 5 and 13.	Hard frost Sept. 8.
1977	Planted veg. garden 3rd week April.	Dry hot April. Snow mid-May.	Hard frost Sept. 27.
1978	Planted veg. garden 1st week May.	Light frost June 6.	Hard frost Sept. 15
1979	Planted veg. garden 2nd week May.	Late, cold spring. Frost first week June.	Hard frost Sept. 29
1980	Planted veg. garden 3rd week April.	Early spring, leaves out April 27.	Hard frost Sept. 25.

From the above, one can see the tremendous differences in the length of the frost-free growing season. In 1976, there were barely 90 days between frosts. While in 1980, an early spring and a late fall gave more than 150 growing days. Of course, at the end of a long growing season, one can only wish thay had had the foresight to plant cucumbers, tomatoes or other frost-tender goodies. How does one judge? Realistically, one has to plan according to the short side of the growing season, somewhere around 90 to 100 days and plant things which will mature accordingly.

The wise gardener in this zone may plant to allow for the two extremes;

a short, cool summer or a long warm one. A flower bed for example might be planted with pansies and snaps which don't mind cool summers and can survive early frosts to bloom during an October Indian summer and with a few things like marigolds and zinnias which thrive in hotter, drier weather.

As we can see from Mrs. Nelson's diary, hot spells in April or May do not necessarily mean a long growing season will follow. Such spells are too often followed by frost or even snow in early summer (June is statistically our wettest month). In one of her last notations, Mrs. Nelson has marked "leaves out April 27". This is an important sign to watch for and far more accurate than watching the calendar or the thermometer. Once the leaves come out on native poplar or willow it *generally* means that a given area is safe from any further hard frosts until fall. For some reason these native plants are not fooled by warm spells in spring during the years when cold weather is still to come.

The time of leaf-out (exfoliation) varies a great deal from year to year and from place to place in the high country of the chinook zone. On the average it occurs between May 15 and 25, a fairly safe time to plant all but the most tender bedding out plants. However, about 2 years out of 10, exfoliation can occur at the end of April. At the other extreme, one year out of ten, the leaves may not come out until the first week in June.

The average date of leafing out is also the best way to determine whether a particular site is in one of the milder or cooler spots of the overall zone. In the most easterly parts of this gardening zone, where the altitude drops and the foothills blend with the plains, the native trees always leaf out earliest and the growing season is therefore a little longer.

The last places to leaf out are in the valleys closest to the alpine forest along the west side of the chinook zone. There are spots where late May or early June is nearly always the time of exfoliation. Sometimes such spots are referred to as 'frost hollows'. It is because cold air, being heavier, flows to the lowest spots. However, because these valleys are often heavily treed, well-sheltered and blessed with richer soils they give the impression of being much warmer.

If one were able to choose the ideal garden site in the high country of the chinook zone, it would be neither too high and wind-blown nor too low and frost prone.

Outdoor Seed Sowing and Transplanting Guide

Although May 24th is used as a wide guideline for the date to sow seeds, in the area covered by our book frost may come at any time of the year, and vary greatly from year to year. Some plants are able to take far more frost than others and the earlier the tough ones are set out or sown the greater use they will make of the extra days to make a good root system. The following timetable works pretty well:

When these are in full bloom:	Sow these:	Plant out these:
Buffalo beans	Lettuce Peas Sweet Peas Poppies	Onions Pansies
Saskatoons	Broad Beans Carrots Turnips Beets Spinach Calendula Clarkia	Petunias Snapdragons Cabbage Broccoli Potatoes
Lilac	Green Beans Corn Zinnias Squashes	Marigolds Lobelia Nemesia Alyssum Tomatoes Salvia Dahlia

Danger times for frost are when the sky clears off after a rain, and at the full moon.

Newspaper or paper of any kind makes a better frost protection than plastic.

 **Helpful Hints**

Water at daybreak on frosty mornings to save plants.

Use rocks to hold heat.

To beat frost sow seeds early and cover with newspaper on cold nights in late May or June. Much easier to cover small plants in spring than big plants in late August eg: corn, beans, zinnias, potatoes.

Chapter Two

Gardening
Management

Soils

The quality of your soil determines to a large extent the range of plants which will be happy in your garden. If you learn to recognize the type of soil you possess, you can work enormous improvements with the addition of amending substances.

The soils in the foothills vary widely in texture and acidity. Roughly speaking, the further west you go the more acid the soil becomes. As the land begins to flatten out to the east and open up into farming country it becomes more alkaline.

Soil should be like a sponge, absorbent with good drainage pores large enough to permit the penetration of air. It should feel springy when walked upon and not pack down too badly after a heavy rain. It should smell clean and fresh and not sour or musty. If it cakes and cracks when the weather is hot and dry, or turns to a sticky bog when wet you have not added enough humus. The word "humus" means virtually any decayed organic matter. If it is not already decayed when you add it to the soil, the bacteria which normally feed the plant roots will be diverted to decay the fresh manure, sawdust, leaves, straw, or whatever you have used as an additive, and will not be available to your plants.

An old *rotted* hay or straw stack bottom is an excellent source of humus with which to improve the texture of your soil. If you are lucky enough to have leaves to rake, these will help a lot if they are dug into the ground. An old gardener's saying is, "Always pay the soil back for what you take out of it." The return of organic matter to the soil is the best way of doing this.

On Facing Page
Top: A good garden needs a wide range of tools.
Centre: Shingles protect new transplants. Plastic holds ground heat and speeds growth.
Bottom: Tomato coldframe, page 21.

The term pH is used to describe the acidity or alkalinity of the soil. It is measured on a scale of one to fourteen. Most plants are happiest near the neutral zone between 6.0 and 8.0.

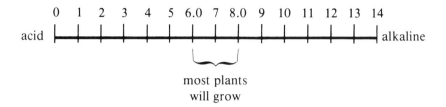

A good household test is to put a teaspoonful of the soil to be tested in a clean saucer and pour on a few drops of vinegar. Vinegar, being acid, will not react with another acid material but when coming into contact with alkali it will fizz and bubble. If your soil erupts like Mt. St. Helen's you have a very alkaline condition. If no reaction at all it is acid. With practice it is possible to tell the degree of alkalinity fairly accurately. If your soil pH is way out of line it will tie up the nutrients in the soil and make them unavailable to the plant.

Having determined the pH of your garden soil, next consider the texture, which is equally important.

Parts of the region have heavy clay soil which is very hard to work unless conditions are perfect. Such soil can be improved by the addition of some coarse sand to break it up a little and promote drainage. Generous application of humus will also help to a large degree. The coarse sand available here is usually very alkaline so remember to watch out for this and correct it if necessary with the addition of sulphur.

The light, shallow, sandy soil found along the river valleys has perfect drainage but will dry out very quickly and leach out all its food value into the underlying gravel if a layer of humus is not dug in each year. Alberta soils in general are very short of humus and it is hard to overdo the application of fibrous matter.

If you've done everything else right and your plants still do not seem to thrive, or if you wish a more scientific measurement of the pH of your soil, send a sample of soil away to your District Agriculturist for analysis. Take samples from several different places in your garden, mix together, and let it air dry before packing in a plastic bag. About two cups is sufficient. Enclose a description of what you want to use the soil for and the current fee for each sample you want tested. It takes about three weeks to get the result but is well worth it when you get a detailed analysis of the texture, pH and nutrient value of the soil in question.

Soil which is too acid is very seldom a problem in this area but if encountered it may be corrected with the addition of some lime. A half-

and-half mixture of dolomite lime and calcium carbonate (the agricultural kind, not the hot or unslaked lime which is sold for outhouses) applied at the rate of one pound per one hundred square feet should help. If on the other hand, your soil is too alkaline you may add sulphur at a maximum rate of one pound per one hundred square feet. Both these chemicals are long-lasting and will not need to be done again for several years. Peat moss will also add acidity to the soil, but has several disadvantages too when added in sufficient quantities to alter the pH. It is very expensive and extremely hard to moisten under outdoor conditions. Only when pre-wetted by thoroughly mixing with hot water does it improve the moisture-holding capacity of the soil and increase the acidity. However, if added dry or if it ever dries out, it tends to repel water rather than attract it, and it contains no nutrients at all. Far better to use compost, or well-rotted manure. Do not use fresh manure or you will burn the roots of the plants and have quite a weed problem. Try to find a source of old black crumbly manure which is practically back to the state of soil again. It can be added in the fall provided it is dug in before freeze up, or early in spring before things start to grow.

Many of our local gardeners are lucky enough to have good, deep, rich, black loam, but even these lucky people will find their soil easier to work and improved in texture if they make generous applications of humus.

When buying loam it is important to ensure that it has not been sprayed with any herbicide within the last ten years or so. 2-4-D persists in the soil over a long period and will be harmful to seedling growth. If you can obtain a sample of soil before you buy it and try to grow something in it, that is the best test. Tomato seedlings are quick to show herbicide contamination. They will develop distorted leaves if any herbicide is present.

A good gardener can pick up a handful of soil, crumble it between his fingers, smell it, and can tell by instinct whether his soil is "in good heart" or not. Gardeners in the old days could tell whether they had to add lime, sulphur, manure, sand, bone meal, etc. without knowing the scientific reason behind it. Although we have lost much of this ancient wisdom, we do have modern science to give guidelines for success and all we have to do is follow the rules.

Fertilizer

Besides soil, water, air and sunlight, plants need nutrients or plant food to grow and produce well. Some of these nutrients are already in the soil depending on how well it has been farmed and taken care of. If the soil has been used a lot without having had anything put back, it will be lacking in plant food and so will only produce weak, sickly plants.

The main plant food elements are:

1. Nitrogen (N) builds plant protein which encourages leaf and stem

Leaves
Nitrogen - For plant protein, rich green leaves.

Flowers
Potash - For growth, superior blooms and disease resistance.

Roots
Phosphate - For plant sugar to develop roots and flowers.

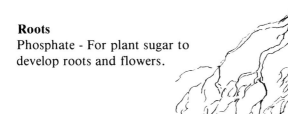

growth, gives rich green colour and rapid growth. It is good for leaf crops and lawns. Too much will burn and kill plants.

2. Phosphorus (P) builds plant sugar which helps to develop roots and flowers. Good for young plants when transplanting. Also good for root crops.

3. Potassium (K) (Potash) - for growth - increases vigour of plants, helps disease resistance and promotes better flowers, seeds and fruit.

Gardeners should always replace these nutrients or plant foods by one of the following:

1. Adding and working into the soil well-rotted manure - cow, horse, sheep or chicken. Cow manure is the safest followed by horse manure. Chicken and sheep manure are much stronger in nitrogen and can burn and kill plants if too much is used. One advantage of sheep manure is

that it is weed free; the rest will usually produce a good crop of weeds. Using manure tea will get away from the weed problem. This is made by soaking well-rotted manure in water and using the water for plants. It will not add any humus to the soil. Place a shovelful of manure in a burlap sack and suspend in a bucket or barrel which is set to catch the heat of the sun. This will keep particles from clogging your watering can. Or, after a rain collect water from puddles in your corrals.

2. Adding compost and working into the soil.

3. Adding and working into the soil; grass clippings, straw, leaves, etc. There is no danger of burning plants with this, but the soil will probably need some fertilizer containing nitrogen and phosphorus as the rotting process of these in the soil uses up some of these elements. However, it will greatly improve the texture of the soil adding humus to make it loose and healthy.

4. Bone meal - contains a lot of phosphorus. Very good for bulbs.

5. Commercial chemical fertilizers all display a formula consisting of three groups of numbers. The first number is the percentage of nitrogen (symbol N). The second number is the percentage of phosphorus (symbol P). The third number is the percentage of potassium (symbol K).

Example: 11-48-0. This fertilizer would contain 11% nitrogen, 48% phosphorus and no potassium, therefore it would be a good fertilizer for root crops.

16-20-0. This fertilizer would contain 16% nitrogen, 20% phosphorus and no potassium and would be a good formula for most gardens.

20-20-20. This fertilizer would contain 20% nitrogen, 20% phosphorus and 20% potassium and would be a good fertilizer for flowering plants.

Apply commercial fertilizer as directed on the container but be on the safe side and use a little less than called for as too much can burn and even kill your plants.

Broadcast fertilizer lightly before spring tilling and seeding. Later on if necessary, add a little more along both sides of the row and work into the soil, or around individual plants. If plants get about two inches high and have enough moisture but look pale, unhealthy and are not growing, they will probably benefit from the addition of fertilizer. also, most garden plants benefit from a light application of fertilizer just before they bloom, produce vegetables or fruit.

Legume crops such as peas and beans produce their own nitrogen so they don't like a fertilizer with a high percentage of nitrogen.

Wood ashes contain lime which, when worked into the garden, react to release the nitrogen in the soil making it available to your plants. They are also a good source of a potassium. Wood ashes are also said to discourage insect pests.

Some gardeners recommend the use of green manure, which is a cover crop, usually oats, barley or rye. It is left to grow only to six or eight inches then turned into the soil. In mild climates the cover crop can be planted as vegetables are removed from the garden. However with our short foothills growing season, it is best to plant where you are summer-fallowing a portion of the garden.

Compost

Compost is an excellent soil conditioner - the water holding capacity of sandy loam is improved greatly by the addition of compost and heavy clay is made more porous by mixing with compost. Compost also provides nutrients to plants over a long period of time in a form that is readily available to them. It also provides trace elements which are not available in commercial fertilizers.

Basically compost is made by the decomposition of organic matter. This can be garden wastes, grass clippings, sawdust, kitchen wastes, and so forth. These are usually built up on a pile with alternate layers of soil. Water and oxygen are essential for decomposition, thus the pile should be regularly turned to supply oxygen to all parts of the pile. It should be moistened when required. To speed up the decomposition process, a compost pile can be covered with black plastic to retain heat and moisture. When compost is ready it smells rather fresh and earthy, is dark in colour and humusy in texture. It usually takes about 6 to 8 weeks in the summer to form but to create compost in this length of time, the use of a commercial rotting agent is often required. Winter's cold temperatures completely halt development of compost. Rotting is limited to the warmest months, but because Alberta is so dry, things often don't rot without assistance during most summers. A good idea is to have three compost piles; one which is being added to, one which is being turned and one which is ready for use.

Herbicides, Insecticides and Fungicides

Indiscriminate and over use of any of these can be very dangerous. They can destroy good plant life, beneficial insects and bird life, as well as poisoning children and pets. They can pollute our water and environment for years to come.

Herbicides check and stop growth of undesirable plants. Insecticides are used to kill insect pests. Fungicides help prevent and control plant diseases. These are all chemicals, their use can be a blessing or a curse. You may say, why use them? There are certain circumstances when one of these chemicals has to be used to control a very bad weed, insect or plant disease, which if not controlled, will take over your property and spread to your neighbour's. These undesirables have to be brought under control quickly before they spread and take over. In such a case the safest

14

thing to do is get in touch with your Municipal District fieldman. He will be able to assist you by telling you what to use, how much to use and how to use it. Careful, and knowledgeable use of one of these chemicals can be very advantageous. For example, some of the really bad weeds like toad flax and quack grass have to be controlled with a herbicide. Nothing else will stop them from taking over your property and spreading into your neighbour's. Some insect pests and plant diseases if not checked when they start can also spread rapidly and destroy your garden and again spread to your neighbours.

With the use of the right product as soon as you see a problem start

METRIC CONVERSION TABLE

MEASURING

Metric Millilitres	Tea-Spoon	Table-Spoon	Ounce	Cup	Fluid Measure	Wt.
5 ml. ..	1					
10 ml. ..	2					
15 ml. ..	3	1......	½			
30 ml.		2......	1.....	1/8		
60 ml.		4......	2....	¼		
75 ml.		5......	2½...	⅓		
90 ml.		6......	3.....	3/8		
120 ml.		8......	4.....	½		
150 ml.		10......	5.....	⅔		
180 ml.		12......	6.....	¾		
210 ml.		14......	7.....	7/8		
250 ml.		16......	8.....	1....	½ pt.	
280 ml.		18......	9.....	1-1/8		
360 ml.		24......	12.....	1½..	¾ pt.	
500 ml.			16....	2....	1 pt. ...	1 lb.
750 ml.			24....	3....	1½ pt. .	1½ lb.
1000 ml.			32....	4....	1 qt. ...	2 lbs.
2000 ml.			64....	8....	2 qts. ..	4 lbs.
4000 ml.			128.....	16....	1 gal. ..	8 lbs.

Converting Volume:
pints × .57 = litres
quarts × 1.1 = litres
gallons × 4.5 = litres

Converting Weight:
kilograms × 2.2 = pounds
grams × 0.035 = ounces
pounds × 0.45 = kilograms
ounces × 28 = grams

you can wipe it out, but if left unchecked it will spread and require a lot more treatment to bring under control. So the answer is keep a close watch on your yard for bad or unusual persistant weeds; heavy insect damage; sick, wilting and dying plants, then immediately get help from your district weed and pest control officer to advise you on what to do.

Control of Garden Pests

Identify your enemy before using big guns. Very often if a plant looks sick it immediately gets sprayed with everything at hand. This will often make the plant sicker and you too. A good strong stream of cold water will do more good than anything. Even if you see holes on the leaves make sure your pest is still present and not hatched and gone. There are Plant Pathology Labs at a number of regional centres which will analyze samples and reply very quickly with recommendations and identifications. Very often the problem is a cultural one and not an insect at all.

Our members have used the following ideas to assist them in control of garden pests:

Ants:
- plant mint by your house, especially near the doors, to keep ants out
- pour boiling water over nests
- put up nest boxes for flickers as they love to eat ants

Aphids:
- to repel, plant nasturtiums, marigolds, petunias, garlic and chives throughout your vegetable garden and nasturtiums and petunias under your fruit trees.
- to repel, plant chives with your rose bushes
- ladybugs, green lacewing flies and wasps all eat aphids

Cabbage Butterflies:
- wasps eat eggs of cabbage butterflies
- catch with a butterfly net and destroy
- to repel, plant dill, rosemary, thyme, sage, lavender or mint with crops bothered by cabbage butterflies
- also repelled by marigolds
- use an electric bug zapper
- encourage birds to nest in or near your garden

Cabbage Worms (larvae of adult cabbage butterfly):
- place a heaping tablespoon of wood ashes mixed with earth around the stem of plants bothered by cabbage worms

Colorado Potato Beetle:
- plant green beans beside potatoes to keep beetles off

- to repel, plant horseradish either end of your potato patch, but bear in mind it spreads rapidly
- hand pick and destroy

Cutworms:
- to repel, scatter dampened wood ashes around plants
- Bantam hens and bluebirds love them
- place a tin can from which both ends have been removed around plants and push down in the soil about 2'' to protect from cutworms

Deer:
- fence your garden
- keep a large dog that lives outdoors but don't let your dog run at large or you will have some very unhappy neighbours. If your dog bothers your neighbours' cattle you will probably lose him. It is also against the law for dogs to chase wildlife.
- tie human hair in old nylons and hang it in trees and shrubs around the garden
- 2'' chicken wire mesh laid over perennial beds in winter will stop deer from pawing off winter cover. The same wire laid alongside your raspberry rows in summer will stop deer from eating the canes which they love
- commercial animal repellents

Flea Beetles:
- steep catnip in water, strain and spray on plants
- rotenone dust

Mice, Pocket Gophers (Moles) and Richardson Ground Squirrels (Gophers):
- keep a good cat or dog
- place mothballs in gopher holes which are close to your garden
- dump several scoops of used cat litter down holes of gophers and moles
- plant mint around garden to repel mice
- use a box trap for pocket gophers
- use Victor #0 or #1 traps for gophers
- reputed to be repelled by garlic

Mosquitoes:
- King birds, flycatchers and swallows eat mosquitoes in huge quantities. Encourage these birds by providing water and nest boxes. Dragonflies and wasps also feed on mosquitoes.

Rabbits:
- plant dusty miller around garden to repel rabbits
- are also repelled by garlic, onions and marigolds

Root Maggots:
- to repel, scatter dampened wood ashes around plants
- spread crushed egg shells over soil surface around plants

Slugs:
- pans of beer or saucers filled with vinegar and sugar set level with your soil attract and trap slugs
- place a board in your garden which slugs will hide under during the day. Overturn each day and destroy the slugs which have collected under it.
- soak used grapefruit halves in methyl hydrate, turn over and place a little stick under one side so slugs can crawl under them. Lift in the morning and remove victims.
- remove all decaying debris or any ground cover as well as bottom leaves of cabbages and lettuce.

Spider Mites:
- wash off with a strong stream of cold water
- sulphur lime dormant spray

Rotenone is a reasonably safe insecticide. It should still be used sparingly and with caution as it can upset the natural balance. It helps control cabbage worms, Colorado potato beetle, red turnip beetles, flea beetles and aphids. Insecticidal soap is very effective in controlling mealy bugs, aphids, scale, and caterpillars of all sorts and will not hurt ladybugs. Diatomaceous earth works well against soft bodied insects.

To control egg laying insect pests, till your soil right after harvest to expose eggs to wind and sun which will destroy them. Also, some insects like to lay their eggs on the hard, fall ground - tilling the soil will prevent this.

Practise mid-season feeding with organic fertilizers such as manure tea. To make, steep one part manure in three parts water in a large bucket, Dilute to the colour of weak tea and apply. Remember that healthy plants in a healthy soil usually will not attract pests.

There are various pesticides available to rid your garden of pests, however, improper use of these can cause residues to stay on vegetables grown for human consumption. As well, poisons are non-selective so although they may kill harmful insects they will also kill helpful insects such as ladybugs which eat forty to fifty aphids and mites a day. Furthermore, due to the great risk to children, to household pets, to birds, and to the environment in general, use of these products has become a matter of grave concern.

Is it not better to practise crop rotation, soil improvement, companion planting and other harmless methods of protection? These methods do not always achieve complete success, but neither do the tremendous number of pesticides available on the market today. It has been proven that the more you use them, the more you have to use them which is expensive and time consuming. On the other hand, by using methods such as companion planting you have nasturtiums and marigolds adding happy touches of colour to your vegetable garden and you live with the knowledge that you are doing your small part to ensure a healthy environment for yours and future generations.

Companion Planting

This is a most interesting subject which is fortunately receiving greater attention not only from the general public but from such agencies as the Regional Crops Laboratory at the Alberta Horticultural Research Centre.

It has been observed through time that some insects are repelled by hot colours and that others are repelled by aromatic herbs such as dill and lavender (see preceding section). It has also been discovered that some plants stimulate growth in others, and that still others retard growth. Some of these are listed below:

Do Not Plant:
- carrots with dill
- potatoes near tomatoes
- any of the onion family near peas or beans

Do Plant:
- lettuce with radishes
- tomatoes with parsley
- corn and pole beans with parsley
- broccoli with dill or sage

- carrots with chives
- basil with tomatoes
- peas or beans with corn
- mint with cabbage and tomatoes

Cold Frames

Basically a cold frame is a large box that sits on the ground. They are usually made out of lumber, although they can be made of fibreglass or concrete blocks. Cold frames are covered either with plastic or glass and slope down from the back to the front for the purpose of shedding moisture and receiving more sun. An average cold frame is about eight feet long by four feet wide, three feet high at the back and eighteen inches high at the front. Some gardeners insulate their cold frames with one inch thick styrofoam, for example. Most people build their cold frames next to their house or garage. A southern exposure is best but shade from the hot afternoon sun will be required.

Old storm windows make good cold frame lids as do lids made from clear plastic stretched over a one inch by two inch frame. Lids should be adjustable to allow for good ventilation. During the day the soil in the cold frame is heated by the sun. The heat retained in the soil is given off at night which keeps flats of seedlings warm. If, however, a bad storm is due or a drop in temperature is predicted you should cover your cold frame with blankets and canvas. Some gardeners install a portable heater or a light bulb to provide extra heat to prevent frost from penetrating the frame. Soil heating cables may also be used.

Plants which have been started indoors are placed in cold frames to adjust to outdoor conditions and therefore toughen up before being transplanted directly into the garden. This process is called "hardening off". Sometimes tender, frost-sensitive plants such as squash, cucumbers and tomatoes are grown right inside a cold frame so that on cool nights they can be protected and therefore have a much better chance of reaching maturity.

Cloches

One of our members uses cloches to protect young plants which have been seeded directly in the garden. They are described as follows:

"Each cloche is made from two panels made of one inch by two inch wood which are hinged together. They are eight feet long, eighteen inches

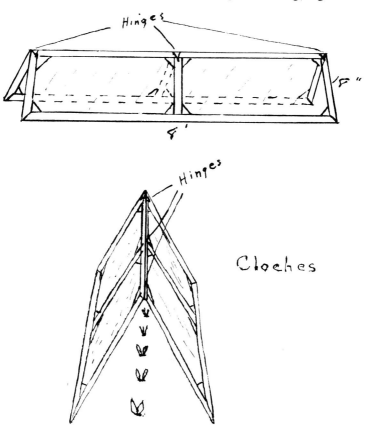

high and their corners are strengthened with plywood gussets. Four mil plastic is stretched over both the inside and the outside of the frames and stapled to them - this creates an insulating air space. They can be folded up flat or opened to form an inverted V. They are used to protect young plants from early spring frosts. Place them over your plant rows inverted V fashion, end to end. At night block the ends to stop the frost from coming in. Open the ends and leave in place during the day. They act as miniature greenhouses. I cover dahlias, corn, potatoes, glads, beans and celery with cloches. They certainly give plants a head start in the spring.''

Tomato Coldframe

by Catherine Laycraft

The frost conditions in some parts of Millarville certainly do not lend themselves to growing tomatoes out in the garden. We have a small coldframe shelter to protect the plants during the cold nights. It is a permanent wooden structure built to fit on a sidehill. The peaked roof is four doors that lift up and are clear fibreglass. The west side and south end are also fibreglass. The north end butts up against the house and on the east side the roof slopes right down to the ground.

Each of the doors is fitted with upright two by fours and nails for locking them at a certain height so that the wind cannot whip them about. When up they provide the plants with ventilation and pure sunlight. This shelter contains no other heat than what it receives and traps from the sun during the day. The plants of course must be watered by a sprinkler as the roof prevents rain from entering. Primarily the project is for the protection of tomatoes, which cannot be left uncovered at night. A simple lowering of the lids is all it takes.

The tomato plants are usually set out about the first of June. However, the coldframe is operational before that. We have planted leaf lettuce, radishes and onions in one section of it and were eating them in May. We have harvested tomatoes as late as October.

 **Helpful Hints**

If you treat your lawn for dandelions DO NOT use the clippings to mulch plants or trees. The chemical will kill or damage them. Do not put these clippings in the compost pile either as the chemical persists. If you have a baby or small children do not use dandelion killer as children can become very ill from playing on treated lawns.

Keep a pair of bantams and family in your garden. They will consume quantities of slugs and insects.

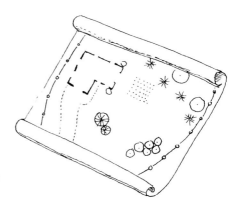

Chapter Three

Landscaping

By Jon Lowry

The principles of good yard and garden design are the same every-where. There is a wealth of excellent books on the market which describe in layman's terms how to construct a workable yard, or a particular feature such as a rockery or patio. Some of these publications are mentioned at the end of this chapter.

However, it is not the purpose of this chapter to duplicate what is already well-explained elsewhere. It is mainly to describe some of the special approaches to landscaping which are known to work well in the high country of the chinook zone.

The Yard Plan

A garden should work for the gardener, not the other way around. When one has to spend every free moment digging weeds or mowing grass, with rarely a chance to flop in a lawn chair and enjoy it all, it usually suggests that the garden has not been properly planned to begin with. Creating a beautiful but easily maintained yard is like a good recipe: a certain number of ingredients and a certain series of steps in putting them together. Miss a step or an ingredient, and you will pay for it in the long run. Oddly enough, the step so many people ignore is the recipe itself; that is, getting a plan down on paper before any construction or planting takes place.

One doesn't have to be an artist or a draftsman to put a plan on paper. Many landscaping and gardening guides explain quite clearly how

On Facing Page

Top: Cotoneaster, a sure bet for fall colour.

Centre: Evergreens in winter.

Bottom: Colour leads your eye to the view corridor. Grape hyacinths give early spring colour.

to go about drawing a plan. There are simply too many variables and possibilities whether trying to improve an older yard or starting upon a new site. A garden plan is not something that can be left to chance or memory. Drawings and notes are essential for the average person to gain a complete picture of what lies ahead.

The first step of any yard plan is to set out the existing features of a site; buildings and established plantings, underground services and overhead wires, important view corridors, wet and dry spots, contours and drainage patterns, traffic patterns, and so on. At this stage the plan is really just an inventory, and a useful exercise in careful observation. It usually comes as a surprise just how many important factors might have been overlooked. Make photocopies of the first drawing and use them to plan what is going to be added.

One can find attractive yards that have never been planned out on paper. They are few in number however, and often the result of having shifted around plantings through several seasons of trial and error. It is much easier to move things around with a pencil and eraser. A plan helps us to see how seemingly insurmountable jobs can be broken into a series of smaller tasks, perhaps staged over several seasons. It helps us to anticipate problems before they occur, such as planting more than can be maintained at a given time. Also, where some aspects of the plan may have to be sub-contracted, it is helpful in keeping track of costs and seeking competitive bids. This way, it is you who control the design and not the contractor.

If the gardener can get to a stage where the plan is at least roughed in and various features indicated on a fairly accurate scale, it pays to take stakes into the garden and use them to represent all the changes and additions proposed. For plantings, tall stakes and bits of scrap lumber can represent trees, and shorter ones can stand for shrubs. Painting the stakes different colours or tying them with coloured rags will help the eye to sort out the different species, or at least to distinguish between which plantings are evergreen (the backbone of every chinook zone garden) and which ones drop their leaves. Red, pink and orange markings can be used to represent the plants that will flower or add touches of fall colour.

When the planting stakes are in place, return to the house and double check to determine what the garden will look like from a favourite armchair or spot by the window. At this stage, a great many possible planting errors are easily detected. For example, it should be possible to see if a particular planting might eventually block an important view corridor or create snow drifting problems on the front walk. Return to the yard, move the stakes around and add or subtract a few until the changes required are completed.

At the same time, it's a good idea to get in a car, drive up to the site and approach it as though you were seeing it through the eyes of a visitor.

24

This may require another set of adjustments. For instance it may become obvious that although you would like visitors to call at the front entrance, the proposed plantings might be hiding that entrance while the brightest or most interesting plantings are inadvertently drawing attention to another entrance.

With planting stakes in place, check also to see what kind of a lawn mowing pattern will result. Some of the biggest maintenance headaches occur when lawn areas are punctuated with too many individual trees and shrubs. If it appears that mowing will mean too much turning, backing up, or passing through tight places then chances are the lawn will never look well-cared for without continuous attention. If the mowing pattern is time-consuming, all other aspects of lawn care such as fertilizing, watering, edging, or raking will be just as difficult. Also, check to see if there are too many spots where the grass runs directly up against walls, fences or other barriers which will need hand trimming to look well-groomed. This is another time-consuming step that can often be eliminated by either creating a planting bed around the obstacle or by installing a wooden 'mowing edge'.

Once again, the stakes which represent plantings may have to be re-arranged to define lawn areas that can be maintained in one easy swoop. This is done by organizing shrubs and trees into groups where each group is maintained as a bed, either to be mulched or cultivated. Whether strictly for shelter or for purposes of enhancement, group plantings somehow always look better than having a number of individual trees and shrubs scattered throughout the lawn area or lined in straight rows. Group plantings also look best, or at least more natural, when each group is limited to just one or two different species. For example, a bed of spruce would be an attractive background for a bed of dogwood. Or, in a two-species bed, a group of sea buckthorn could be bordered and underplanted with Arcadia juniper.

One last thing to watch for when sizing up the garden during the planning and staking out stage is the slopes. Any slope which is less than 3 times longer than it is high will make a poor lawn; firstly because slopes are awkward to mow and, secondly, because it requires too much watering in our dry climate to keep them green. Though it takes more time in the initial planting or construction stages, low maintenance is the result whenever slopes are terraced and converted to plantings of ground covers or shrubs. Species which work well on slopes are listed in Chapter Six.

For the beginner or the average home gardener to achieve professional-looking results, any constructed feature of a garden must also be marked with stakes, *and* outlined with string before one nail is pounded or one spadeful of dirt is moved. This applies to decks, pathways, fences and screens, benches, garden steps, retaining walls and so on. Stakes are used to mark corners and posts, but the string is essential in allowing the gardener to see and imagine how the edges and tops of constructed features will actually end up. A string can be quickly wrapped around a line of nails punched into the earth when trying to visualize and lay out the edges of pathways and beds.

When this has been done, again it is very easy to walk around, visualize the finished product from different angles, spot potential flaws in the design, and make the necessary changes. One might see where the railing on a deck has to be raised or lowered to expose a good view. Or, it may become obvious that a walkway is too narrow or not lying where people are most apt to walk. One might also see where construction problems could occur, where a sharp corner poking out might create a hazard, where a tight space might be hard to plant or maintain.

Stakes and string are a necessary preliminary part of almost any type of construction. Apart from helping to troubleshoot errors in design they provide a last chance to make purely aesthetic changes before construction begins. For example, the average person is most apt to think in terms of straight lines and 90 degree angles, and there's no question that this is the easiest way to build. There are, however, a number of shapes other than squares and rectangles which lend themselves better to the natural lines of a garden, and which can be easily built using straight line materials.

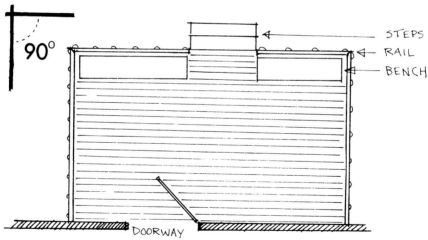

Imagine how much softer it looks to cut the two square outside corners off a deck using a 45 degree turn instead. By installing a bench and rail that turns in the same way, one can create a comfortable and useful conversation area around a small table. At the same time, beyond the deck in the space that would have been filled by a rather useless square corner, a shrub can be planted which will help to visually anchor the deck or screen it from the wind.

26

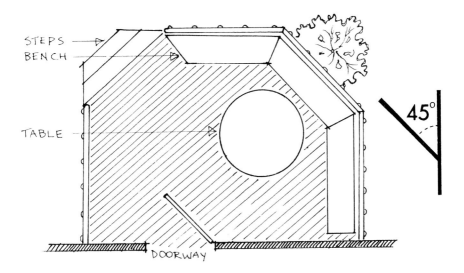

STEPS
BENCH

TABLE

45°

DOORWAY

The 45 degree turn can also be applied to sidewalks wherever there is a tendency for people to shortcut across a square turn. Again, it looks better and saves trying to revive a worn patch of lawn or a bunch of battered bedding plants.

Once we take the step from thinking only in terms of 90 degree corners to substituting 45 degree turns, it becomes easier to go even further and begin using curves and undulations to enhance the visual flow of the garden. Consider how the fence which is designed to enclose or avoid a group of trees or shrubs is usually far more pleasing to look at than one which cuts straight through.

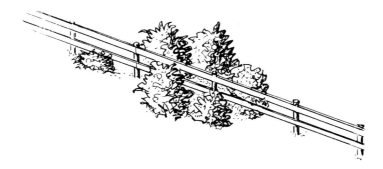

Note on this and the next page how the same posts and the same straight boards, gently angled, give the illusion of a curve which actually helps to draw attention to the planting. The same principle, that is, using straight materials to produce the effect of curves, has unlimited application in creating more attractive landscapes. The straight path or

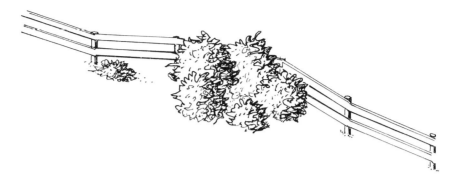

retaining wall at the foot of a rounded bank conflicts with the shape of the bank. Rounding the constructed features to fit the shape of the bank enhances both the bank *and* the path or wall. Where a straight mowing edge around the foundation planting of a house would actually exaggerate the squareness of the building in an 'unsquare' environment, a curved mowing edge will instead serve to blend the house with its surroundings. Straight lines in both planting and construction are especially unattractive in flat or monotonous terrain. On a long narrow lot, any straight line running down the length of the property, whether it's a planting or a fence, or both, will only make the site look even narrower.

Though these principles of line and shape may seem foreign to the beginner, they do become much clearer once a site has been marked out with stakes and string. Whether one has to erase and redraw a plan over and over, or spend days arranging and rearranging stakes, it always pays off in the end.

Spacing

In the most rigorous gardening areas it is human nature to try to grow as many kinds of things as possible and to plant as much as energy allows. Overplanting is one of the major pitfalls for the enthusiastic beginner. Not only is it the easiest trap to fall into, it is the one we pay for most dearly in the long run. Overplanting happens for a number of reasons. It may be the desire for fast results in a garden which appears too drab and empty. Perhaps it is an effort to compensate for what appears to be a lack of colour or variety in a zone with a very long dormant season. Or, as is often the case, overplanting is simply the failure to foresee the ultimate size and shape of seedlings or juvenile plants.

The overplanted garden is a tangled mess and a maintenance headache. Wherever different species of trees and shrubs crowd each other they become distorted and can never exhibit the beauty of their individual natural shapes. It is often very difficult to maintain the overplanted garden because weeds creep into places where the gardener cannot reach to remove them. The competition for space and light also generates a great deal of deadwood and diseased plant material. One is forever sawing, clipping and burning in the overplanted garden.

Whenever the gardener puts off thinning out crowded areas, or realizes too late that culling and removal of certain plants is necessary, the problem only compounds itself. The bigger trees and shrubs become the harder they are to remove and the less likely it is that they can be transplanted and recycled successfully in another part of the garden. Where woody plants have been left to grow for several seasons in a crowded situation, removing some specimens leaves behind others which are misshapen. It may take years for the remaining specimens to recover their natural shape and hide the scars and gaps of overplanting.

Basically there are two approaches to spacing of plantings depending on the desired effect. If the object is to create a grouped effect where several plants of the same species are intended to grow into a grove or clump, small shrubs can be planted 3-4 feet apart, large shrubs 6-8 feet, and trees 10-12 feet. In a town or city garden, for example, one corner of the yard could contain a group planting of potentilla or dogwood. On larger properties, old favourites like honeysuckle or lilac shrubs look good grouped together or planted as an informal hedge. Acreage gardens also have room for groups of spruce, or pine or even poplar arranged with like things together as they often grow in the wild. A medium size tree which lends itself well to group planting is the laurel leaf willow.

When different species are planted side by side the spacing should be more generous so that each specimen can achieve its ultimate size and natural shape unhindered and undistorted and without need of corrective pruning. For example, a mixed planting of large trees such as spruce and poplar will require a minimum spacing of 16 feet between specimens, and as much as 20 feet if one has the space. Larger growing shrubs such as mugho pine and honeysuckle should be kept 10-12 feet apart if it is intended that each individual specimen will stand out on its own.

When setting out markers or small plants, these distances and the gaps between them can seem enormous. It takes a great deal of restraint not to move things closer together or fill the gaps with additional trees or shrubs. However, it is important to let patience prevail to the point where one actually begins to appreciate watching things fill out and gain substance as the years fly by. If a new planting of tiny trees and shrubs seems entirely too sparse in the first 2 or 3 seasons, one can always fill the empty spaces with annuals, perennials or ground covers.

Extending the Illusion of Summer

In a region where trees are in leaf for little more than four months and grass stays green not much longer, most people find it desirable to break the monotony of bieges and greys which predominate in the long dormant season. Therefore, the best planned gardens in this zone start with strong emphasis on evergreen plantings; from one-third to one-half in major focal points of the yard. As much as another third should comprise species that make it seem as though spring arrives a little bit earlier and fall lingers later:

Plants which leaf out early:

Gooseberry	Mayday
Red Elder	Chokecherry
Cherry prinsepia	Willow

Plants which hold leaves late or show bright fall colour:

Laurel leaf willow	Lilac
Cotoneaster	Royalty crabapple
Mountain Ash	

Plants which are attractive all seasons:

Trees	**Shrubs**
Pine	Red Leaf Rose
Spruce	Dogwood
Weeping birch	Golden ninebark
	Sagebrush
Ground Covers	Euonymus Turkestan
Bergenia	Highbush cranberry
Kinnikinick	Sea buckthorn
Wintergreen	Juniper
Snow in Summer	

Planters for Winter Beauty

When nurseries clear out their potted stock in fall, it's an ideal time to buy small evergreens cheaply. Certain kinds can add a touch of life to an otherwise empty planter throughout the winter. Kept moist during any winter dry spells, the following will normally survive one or more years until its time to plant them in the ground. Mugho pine and Colorado spruce are the toughest of the imported species for this purpose. All native evergreens, spruce, pine and juniper, also work well. Avoid other non-native evergreens and junipers in ordinary planters or containers, as they will rarely survive past mid-February in this climate zone.

Except for those recommended above, most evergreens and woody plants do poorly in winter if the roots are subjected to the kind of extreme and repeated freezing and thawing that effects the *soil* of aboveground tubs and planters. In the chinook belt, a special type of constructed planter can minimize this problem and greatly improve the possibilities for adding winter colour. The key is to provide for insulation of the root zone. A double-walled planter which meets this requirement is pictured on the colour page of Chapter 16. As diagrammed below, such units are often attached to buildings (for illusions of width, to hide a too-high foundation, or to provide a planter/bench), but they can also be built tub style. Because insulation will not work if it becomes moist, either the inside wall should be made water tight or styrofoam insulation used.

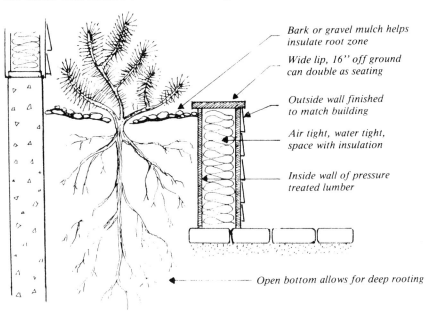

Bark or gravel mulch helps insulate root zone

Wide lip, 16" off ground can double as seating

Outside wall finished to match building

Air tight, water tight, space with insulation

Inside wall of pressure treated lumber

Open bottom allows for deep rooting

Recommended Reading
Reader's Digest Practical Guide to Home Landscaping. A Canadian edition with 460 well-illustrated pages. Covers most common planning problems in rural and urban gardens from beginning to end, with lots of do-it-yourself solutions. Zone classification for tree and shrub hardiness is inaccurate with regard to our area and should be supplemented by the plant recommendations in the Alberta Horticultural Guide.

Landscaping Your Home. Revised Edition by Wm. R. Nelson Jr., can be ordered through the University of Illinois at Urbana-Champaign, College of Agriculture, Cooperative Extension Service. Refer to Circular 1111. Excellent, readable discussion of working with various shapes and lines with dozens of drawings and examples. Hardiness classification of trees and shrubs is not applicable to the chinook zone, but this is a very minor flaw in a good, inexpensive book.

Low Maintenance Gardening, one of several Sunset books which cover various aspects of landscaping, this one has page after page of tried-and-true solutions to common maintenance problems, well-explained with a number of before and after drawings.

Chapter Four

Trees, Shrubs and Roses

Trees and Shrubs
by Anne Vale

Hardy Varieties

The chinooks are a limiting factor in growing many varieties otherwise hardy on the prairies. Trees and shrubs with a low dormancy rate can be triggered into growth by spells of warm weather, only to be zapped when the temperature falls back to winter levels. Dryness of soil and air is another obstacle to successful growing of many varieties.

However don't be discouraged. There are many different choices of shapes, sizes and textures to try. As a good rule of thumb those marked with a "c" for "chinook" in the Alberta Horticultural Guide are worth a try. This booklet is available from your District Agriculturalist, or through the Department of Agriculture in Edmonton. Further on in this chapter a list of suggested trees and shrubs for varied locations is given.

Siting

Fences, buildings, shelter belts, natural contours; all can create mini-climates where you may have success with an otherwise borderline hardy shrub. A grouping of shrubs together can collect a good insulating snow drift and low lying spots collect rain water and snow melt to help those trees which prefer more moisture. Save the high spots and thin sandy soil for those shrubs which are drought resistant. This is explained more fully in the chapter on landscaping.

On Facing Page

Top: This rose bush has been growing in the Millarville area for over 60 years.

Bottom: Variety and contrast in foliage colour creates visual interest. Two blue spruce frame a purple-leafed Shubert chokecherry at the base of which sits a native sagebrush. In the foreground, bottom, a native and an imported juniper intermingle with snow-in-summer.

Time of Planting

I prefer to plant as early in the spring as possible. I do not recommend fall planting in this area although some members have had success with this method. In the spring the plant has everything going for it, but in fall it is doubtful whether the plant will have time to become established before an Alberta winter sets in.

Methods of Planting

Trees to be dug up and transplanted must be moved in a dormant condition before they get leaves. Never leave the roots drying in the air while you dig the new hole. If it has to be dug before its permanent site is ready, put it in a large pot or garbage bag with some soil and keep it well watered until you can plant it.

When planting trees and shrubs which have already leafed out it is important not to disturb the roots. Trees are purchased from garden centres in many different kinds of containers. The biodegradable pots, such as compressed peat, tar paper, or wooden baskets, may be planted intact except for slashing the sides and peeling back the rim. If you leave the rim of the pot sticking out it will act as a wick and draw the moisture out of the soil. More permanent containers must of course be removed but take care not to disturb the root ball. If the plant has leaves already

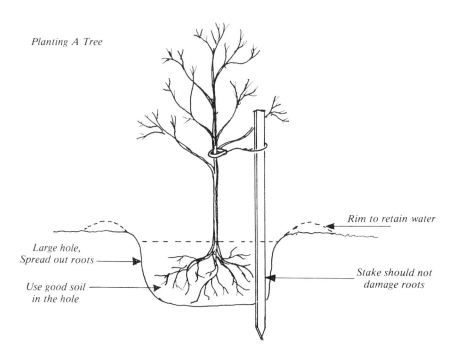

Planting A Tree

Rim to retain water

Large hole,
Spread out roots

Use good soil
in the hole

Stake should not
damage roots

it needs the fine root hairs to replace moisture lost by transpiration into the air from the leaf surface.

Larger trees planted with a tree mover should have a bigger hole than the tree plug dug first and partly filled with a muck or a mud slurry before receiving the tree so that the roots have somewhere to go. All cracks should also be filled with a slurry. Larger trees should always be guy-wired for the first 3 years to prevent wind blowing them over. Thread the wire through pieces of old hose to prevent chafing of the tree.

Smaller trees planted by hand should have a hole dug at least twice the size of the root ball. The bigger the hole the better your chance of success.

Taller trees should be staked for a few years until established. A rim of soil around the edge of the hole will retain water until it has had a chance to soak in. The plant should be kept thoroughly and deeply watered throughout its first few years until it has a good root system. Lawn sprinkling is not sufficient to water deeply planted trees. This will only encourage shallow roots waiting near the surface for the next hand out.

Fertilizer

The time to fertilize your trees and shrubs is early in the spring of their second and subsequent years. Use a fertilizer high in phosphorus (10-52-10 for example). This will stimulate root growth and once you have a good root system then the top half will follow naturally and not be forced into lush growth before the roots can provide sufficient nourishment. I do not recommend fertilizer at planting time with either chemicals or manure. It is easy to be heavy handed with the fertilizer in the attempt to get a good start and burn the tiny roots which are trying to form. If you feel you must do something try an old trick and put a small shovelful of oats or barley in the bottom of the hole. These will ferment and the heat from this process will encourage roots to form. They also provide a seal between the root ball and the wall of the hole.

Winter Care

As late in the year as you can run the hose, water the young trees and shrubs deeply and thoroughly. This will ensure that they freeze deep down and that they do not dehydrate over the winter. Also, on a warm day in late fall use an anti-desiccant spray on your trees to protect them from drying winds in winter. In a warm spell in winter water them again, hose down the branches and make sure the soil is wet and will freeze. If you want to mulch them wait until after freeze up. A mulch which prevents the ground from freezing is an open invitation to mice to move in and take up residence for the winter. They particularly like a nibble of fresh bark and will totally ring-bark and kill many valuable plants. A rodent repellant may be painted on the bottom of the trunk.

Pruning

This district is no different to any other for following the rules for good pruning.

The basic objects of pruning are to achieve (a) a natural shape, (b) to maintain the health and vigour of the plant and, (c) to keep it to a manageable size. Cuts should be made cleanly and as close to the trunk or limb as possible so as not to make an amputated-looking stub. Large wounds should be painted with a tree wound dressing to stop bleeding and prevent the entry of disease organisms. You should remove any dead or diseased wood and also any branches which cross over or rub on each other before they get too big. Try to avoid making the whole tree look as if it has had a bad hair cut by carefully selecting which branch to remove or shorten without spoiling the shape of the tree.

Not all trees like to be pruned at the same time of year. This is fortunate as it spreads the work load out over slack times of year.

When to Prune:

Flowering shrubs: Should be pruned immediately after flowering to give them time to make buds for next year. If you prune them in spring you will remove all the blossom.

Deciduous trees: May be done at any time in winter when they are dormant, with the exception of birch, which should be done in June or July.

Roses: Should be pruned in early May. (See section on roses)

Pines: Mugho pines should have their candles (extended buds) snapped in half in early June to keep them dwarf and bushy. Taller kinds with long needles do not need much pruning and are best left alone.

Spruces: Rarely need pruning. If absolutely necessary prune in July.

Junipers: Prune in July when annual growth is complete. Use great care to make each cut from underneath each branch to leave a natural leader as the right hand diagram shows:

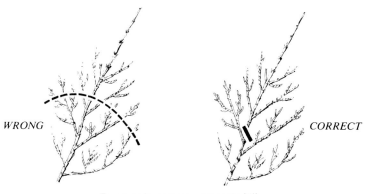

WRONG   *CORRECT*

To prune juniper or remove tip kill.

Recommended Reading: *Woody Ornamentals for Prairie Provinces; The Pruning Manual* by R.H. Knowles, Pub. 1505, Canadian Department of Agriculture; and the *Alberta Horticulture Guide* are excellent booklets which are available through your District Agriculturalist at the Department of Agriculture.

Trees and Shrubs for Special Locations and Purposes:

Sandy Soil

Caragana	Potentilla	Cherry Prinsepia
Sea Buckthorn	Juniper	Pines

Hot Dry Locations

Caragana	Sea Buckthorn
Cotoneaster	Pines
Potentilla	Rocky Mountain Juniper (*scopulorum*)

Heavy Soils

Dogwood	Spruce	Poplar
Lilac	Prunus	Spirea
Roses	Crabapples	
Honeysuckle	Willows	

Shady Locations

Honeysuckle	Dogwood	Mockorange
Red Elder	Alpine Currant	Alpine Fir
Mountain Ash	Hawthorn	
Viburnum	Juniper	

Low Wet Spots

Willow	Dogwood	Birch
Spruce	Spirea	

Coloured Leaves All Summer

Reds	**Yellows**	**Silvers**
Shubert Chokecherry	Golden Plume Elder	Western Sandcherry
Royalty Crab	*Golden Dogwood	Silver Willow
*Purple Leaf Plum	Golden Ninebark	*Silver Dogwood
Red Leaf Rose	Golden Elder	Buffaloberry
		*Russian Olive
		Sea Buckthorn

*Borderline Hardiness

Good Fall Colour

Cotoneaster	Dogwood	Gooseberry
Highbush Cranberry	Saskatoon	Spirea, Anthony
Golden Plume Elder	Chokecherry	Waterer
Red Elder	Mountain Ash	May Day

Those to Bring the Birds

Cotoneaster	Chokecherry	Green Ash - Female
Crabapple	Highbush Cranberry	Most shrubs with berries
Saskatoon	Mountain Ash	

Hedges

Caragana, pygmy	Lilac, Villosa	Potentilla
Cotoneaster	Red Leaf Rose	Alpine Currant
Honeysuckle	Manchurian Elm	

Foundation Planting

This is a confusing term which could mean anything from the foundation of a collection of shrubs to your grandmother's girdle. In actual fact it refers to the type of shrubs which are suitable to plant right up against the foundation of your house, being neither too tall nor too bushy nor needing too much moisture.

Juniper	Russian Almond	Roses
Mugho Pine	Prunus	Spirea
Globe Caragana	Blue Haven Juniper	

Vines

Clematis Jackmanii	Hops	Bittersweet
Clematis Tangutica	Dropmore Honeysuckle	Virginia Creeper

Transplanting Wild Trees and Shrubs
by Jon Lowry

There is never any worry about hardiness or adaptability when planting with trees and shrubs which are native to a given area. This is exactly how the art of gardening began some thousands of years ago. A large proportion of native plants is about the best way to achieve the 'natural look' so often preferred around country homes.

Within a 100 mile radius of the Millarville area are wild species of nearly every plant family that has found a welcome place in temperate zone gardens the world over. The range and variety is so great that, if one has the patience, it is entirely possible to create a tremendously beautiful garden using nothing but native plants. A list at the end of this chapter shows that we needn't limit our choice only to native white spruce nor our excursions only to the nearby forest areas.

When to go Digging

The best time to transplant wild things coincides with what nurserymen call the "bare root" planting season. This is when the trees are without leaves, but the frost is out of the ground. It takes place in both spring and fall and, depending on the year, the period may last from 10 days to 6 weeks on either end of summer. Best results occur when things can be dug and replanted during a spell of cool, misty weather. Woody plants moved in spring have the advantage of a full growing season to readjust and ready themselves for winter. Fall transplanting is most successful when done early enough, say, just as the leaves are falling. This way, in most years, the plants will have several weeks to send out a few new roots before the ground freezes.

A high survival rate of 90% or better also depends on careful digging and transport, and almost immediate replanting. So, plan to dig only as much as can be replanted within 24 hours and don't set out to dig until the planting spot at home has been made ready first. Small items, like foot-high spruce or seedlings of juniper or other ground covers, can simply be lined out in the vegetable garden for a couple of years, and eventually transplanted again to a permanent spot when they get more substance to them. Otherwise, for any tree or shrub in the 4 to 8 foot range there should be a hole ready which is about 30 inches across and 18 inches deep. Beside each hole, have a pile of soil mix, something to mulch with, and stakes and wire. At the least, if there is any chance you'll not have the time or energy to quickly replant the larger specimens, prepare a trench or a pile of wet sawdust where they can be heeled in and stored safely for long periods.

What to Bring
The following is a checklist of useful paraphernalia to bring along on a successful digging expedition:
- a permit allowing removal of plant material
- sharp pruning clippers
- a sharp, long-handled, round-nosed shovel
- wheelbarrow
- plastic garbage bags
- squares of burlap about 4' x 4', predampened
- shiny 2 inch nails
- a tarpaulin, if truck box has no sides or cover
- thick-soled boots, insect repellent, a map, a full tank of gas and a hearty lunch

Pruning Back
Once you have found a suitable specimen within wheelbarrow distance of the truck, use the clippers to clear away any underbrush so that it will be easy to dig from from all sides. Also, for easier digging and a higher chance of survival, prune the specimen itself. For deciduous trees and shrubs don't be afraid to remove from one-half to three-quarters of the top growth and any branches which are flopping on the ground where you will be digging. This is often the hardest step for the inexperienced.

39

However, remember that the volume of stems and branches should nearly equal the volume of root material you'll be able to carry. A 5 foot shrub left unpruned with a one gallon root ball will either die or prune itself by branches dying off in a haphazard manner. On the other hand, after hard pruning, it will produce vigourous new growth which has a more even shape. Spruce, pine and fir do not require such extensive pruning because they can feed off themselves while establishing new roots. Simply remove the oldest branches; the bottom 2 or 3 layers. These can be removed from 6 to 15 inches above ground level depending on the size of the evergreen.

How to Dig a Firm Root Ball

With a shovel, begin cutting, not digging, a ring around the specimen about 10 inches or a foot from the stem. Note that the *back* side of the shovel blade must face the stem and that this first cut is almost straight down. This is the only way to end up with a root ball that holds together until it can be wrapped. A sharp shovel should easily sever all the main surface roots. If hitting a great many large stones at this stage, it is better to tamp in the cuts and move on to another specimen in better soil.

Clear away underbrush & clip branchlets.
Make first cut all around.

Once this thin cut has ringed the specimen, the shovel may be turned to a normal digging position to begin removing dirt. This means digging a second ring about a foot further out, angling inward and downward toward the first cut. As each chunk of sod comes out, it should be piled neatly in one spot so the hole can easily be refilled when the specimen is finally removed. After the first trench has been completed around the tree or shrub, turn the shovel backwards again and repeat the cutting step; this time deeper, in a slightly angled position and closer to the center of the ring. Then dig again to remove dirt and deepen the trench.

40

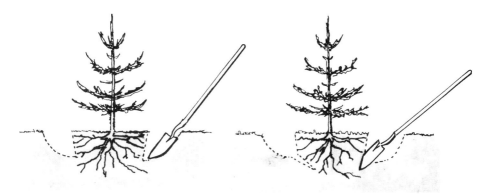

Turn shovel, dig and remove soil.   *Turn shovel, make second cut, then dig again.*

After having made 2 or 3 circuits of cutting and digging, the trench should be from 14 to 18 inches deep. At this point it should be possible to slip the shovel, right side up, completely under the specimen by pressing and cutting, but without prying from several sides of the ring until any tap root and all lower roots are entirely severed.

It usually takes 2 strong backs to carefully lift this size root ball on to a square of burlap. Lift the ball itself and grab the stem only for balance or support. Before wrapping, use the clippers on any main roots that are torn or shredded or poking out too far beyond the root ball. Cut back cleanly to the undamaged parts to promote rapid healing. If your shovel has been well-sharpened most roots will have been cleanly cut. Note that it is more important to retain the finer roots and hair roots. These, rather than the main roots, are what will nourish the plant and produce most of the new root growth when the plant is re-establishing itself. That is the whole point of digging and retaining a solid root ball.

Wrapping

To wrap the ball, pull opposite corners of the burlap toward each other. If long enough, the corners can be tied around the base of the stem. Smooth, shiny nails are used like straight pins to close all the gaps and fasten the burlap to itself until the root ball is completely wrapped. Nails that are rusty or coated with a dull finish will not slip through the fabric easily enough to be of any use. The point of the nail is woven through, against the direction of the pull on the burlap; and, the tighter it is stretched the better it all holds together. Once this technique is mastered, it goes quickly. A well-dug, well-wrapped root ball can bounce around on rough roads without disintegrating.

After wrapping, whenever the specimen is lifted and moved it should be handled by the root ball and by holding on to the burlap. Otherwise, if it is wrongly lifted by holding on only at the base of the stem, large chunks of soil and hair roots will fall away from the stubs of the main roots. If a lot of loose dirt can be felt inside the wrapping it has either been lifted wrongly, set down too hard, or the soil was too rocky and dry to begin with.

Wrap root ball, refill and smooth out hole.

Why Burlap?

At the present time, the Bonar & Bemis sack factory near the Calgary Brewery sells scraps of burlap quite cheaply, by the pound. Burlap acts something like peat moss. When completely dry it does not take up water easily. However, once it is thoroughly soaked it is very slow to dry out and can keep a root ball happily moist longer than other materials. If the burlap squares are presoaked and still damp when used for wrapping, the root ball will quickly soak up more water and hold it like a sponge without making a quagmire in the bed of the truck. Pour a little water on each ball once it's been lifted from the wheelbarrow to the tailgate. If watered before lifting, the balls will be heavier to handle. The other main advantage of using burlap is that it's porous and biodegradable. The root ball can be planted, burlap and all, without having to unwrap and further disturb the roots. Any knots at the neck of the tree should be loosened after planting.

Loading and Hauling

Once watered and sitting on the tailgate, slide the biggest plants forward to sit behind the cab, and balance the truck. Anything taller than 3 feet should be tilted backwards so that nothing sticks above the level of the roof of the cab. Instead of laying them right down where the branches get stomped on, they can be firmly positioned at an angle by lining them up to rest the lower trunk of the ones in front on the root ball of the ones behind.

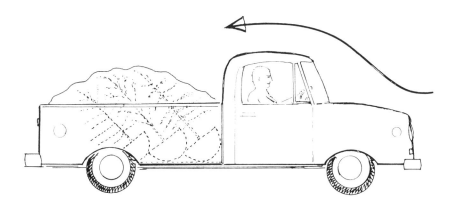

If the truck doesn't have sideboards or a camper shell, then the plants must be covered with a well-fastened tarpaulin. The strong wind current of a moving vehicle is enough to kill many plants which are already in a state of shock. The only exception is when things are hauled in the open air on a cool rainy day, for no more than a few miles at very slow speeds.

Where to Dig:

Many gardeners wonder if it is important when transplanting evergreens to tag the south side of the tree before it's dug and make sure it is facing the same direction when planted. The experts seem to be split on whether orientation makes any difference. What *is* important in the chinook zone, with evergreens especially, and all other trees, shrubs, or ground covers, is to find specimens in conditions that most closely duplicate the site to which they will be moved. For a site where the terrain or the presence of existing trees provides good shelter, one does not have to be as fussy about where transplants originate. However, someone with a more open site should allow for more time and trouble to search out plants not only of the right size for digging but from equally exposed locations. If not, plants taken from sheltered areas to exposed areas will either die, or look so terrible for so long while they readapt, that transplanting is hardly worth the effort.

Everyone's first choice for digging native plant material is usually the forestry area of the foothills. Alberta Forest Services allows such digging with some common-sense restrictions based on just how much the average person can transplant successfully without despoiling the forestry area. A permit must be purchased from any ranger station or Forest Services office during normal business hours, Monday to Friday. So, it is important to obtain a permit in advance if planning to dig on a weekend.

The permit allows for removal of up to 20 specimens per year at a current charge of $1.50 apiece. There are restrictions as to how far from the right-of-way one can dig, and for trees, a maximum size that can be taken. Everything must be dug by hand. On weekdays, when forestry personnel are not overly busy policing crowds of visitors, they can sometimes direct gardeners to the best digging spots and especially to areas which are due to be cleared for road construction. Do not hesitate to ask for advice as it can save a great deal of searching.

On private land, it always pays to ask permission for access. The landowner will know best just what grows where and in heavily wooded areas may even have spots that he or she would like cleaned out. In the semi-desert zone, most farmers and ranchers are downright delighted to get rid of anything which interferes with grazing, such as cactus, sagebrush, potentilla or silver-leafed buffaloberry. Generally, the farther one gets from centres of population, the more likely it is that the landowner will allow removal of plant material. Anyone who refills their holes and smoothes them out is usually welcome to return. It also helps to bring along something to trade; some extra bedding out plants or a potted ornamental tree or shrub.

On public land, road allowances and ditches, it seems that every county and municipality has different rules with respect to the practice of removing wild plant material. Before setting out, it is important to check with the district agriculturist or agricultural fieldman in the area where one intends to dig. In heavily wooded areas, roadside trees and shrubs will grow to become hazardous to traffic, block drainage or interfere with snow removal. The county or municipality may want such growth removed since it will eventually have to be destroyed or poisoned anyway. On the other hand, in the semi-desert zone where soils are extremely light, woody plants actually prevent the roadsides from eroding and their removal is discouraged. In all rural areas where the ditches are used as bridle paths it is a poor and dangerous practice to dig and leave large holes unfilled. Wherever unconscientious plant collectors leave too many holes in popular digging areas, the removal of plant material is often prohibited.

It is unlawful to remove plants from national and provincial parks or from Indian reservations.

What to Dig:
The following is a list of native plant material which is known to transplant well:
Large Evergreen Trees:
White Spruce: the most commonly sought and most successfully transplanted by the beginner. The absence of a true taproot and a web of shallow anchoring roots call for a wide, flat root ball. If the tree suffers transplant shock it may turn a sickly green for one or two seasons, but will eventually regain its deep blue-green colour on new growth once the roots are sufficiently re-established.

Lodgepole Pine: sometimes misnamed as "jackpine", (the true Jack Pine grows further north in the boreal forest zone) this species will add a touch of bright green to the background of any landscape from fall through spring whenever the temperature climbs above freezing. The beginner should try specimens no taller than one metre with a trunk no thicker than a broom stick at the base. For sure-fire success, the hair roots must never be allowed to dry out for even a few seconds during digging, moving and replanting. Like all species of pine, these are especially sensitive to being transplanted and will not withstand some of the abuses which a spruce could tolerate. The root ball should be rounder and deeper to catch as much of the taproot as possible.

Douglas Fir and Balsam Fir: are among the most difficult to move from the wild because it is uncommon to find them growing in the kinds of fine soil which produces a good root ball. Stick to knee-high specimens, and handle them as carefully as pines. They are slow growing but long-lived.

Large Deciduous Trees:

Poplar: There are several types which grow wild in and around the foothills area and they go by names like cottonwood, balsam poplar and balm-of-Gilead, (bomagilian). For use in the garden, it is best to find male specimens because the females drop large amounts of cottony seeds which can be a nuisance on the lawn and planting areas. The earliest catkins indicate male trees and are red in colour.

These often reproduce when surface roots near the parent tree send up shoots or suckers which become trees in themselves. So, when attempting to dig a specimen of broom-handle diameter in or near a grove of poplar, the shovel will strike the large surface root which is feeding it. Even if you are able to sever such a root with an axe, chances are there will not be enough hair roots in the root ball to nourish the specimen through the first season in the garden. It is best to look for a small specimen which has come up from seed on its own.

Medium-Sized Deciduous Trees:

Aspen: Although these can be a striking garden accent, singly or as a group, one rarely sees them being transplanted. Compared to the other kinds of poplar previously mentioned, they are shorter lived and more prone to a number of diseases. Also, aspen is even more likely to spread by root suckering which makes it very difficult to dig a good root ball with a high proportion of hair roots. If you want aspen in the garden, they can be grown most easily by planting finger-sized chunks of root.

NOTE: As wild poplar and aspen have many drawbacks we recommend using modern hybrid trees such as Northwest Poplar or Brooks #6 - male species only.

Black Birch: The only type of birch easy to find in the chinook zone, this multiple-trunked tree usually grows in woodland along creeks and the bottom of gullies. It has a striking silhouette which stands out well against a blank wall or an unconfused background. For successful transplanting try to find a seedling-size specimen and/or by pruning, make sure the volume of above-ground growth nearly equals the volume of roots in the root ball.

Black birch never grows taller than a one-storey house and is one of the few things which can thrive in boggy or poorly drained parts of the yard. In a drier spot they will need a lot of water. This pretty tree does not sucker.

Chokecherry and Saskatoon: will grow into tall shrubs or small trees. Some gardeners use these either for their spring flowers, edible berries, or fall foliage colours which in some, but not all years, can be quite striking. Such ornamental traits are often more pronounced once these are brought into the garden and properly nourished. As with poplar, the trick is to find wild specimens which are not overly large or greatly interconnected with the roots of other specimens in the same clump. Try for lots of finer roots and above-ground growth about the thickness of a pencil.

Shrubs:

Eleagnus commutata: locally known as silver willow, wolf willow or silverberry. This species is closely related to, and makes a good substitute for Russian olive, a common ornamental on the Prairies which is not hardy in the higher country of the chinook zone. The silver leaves make a striking foliage accent with darker things like evergreens or any of the purple-leaved ornamental hybrids. Some gardeners use them for the strong, sweet scent given off by the small yellow flowers in June. These can be planted as a clump, just as they grow in the wild, or easily trained into a small accent tree. Transplanting instructions are the same as for saskatoon. If you cultivate around them they will spread, but surrounded by grass they seem to stay put.

Gooseberry: a greatly under-rated, low, spreading shrub with excellent ornamental qualities. These are a harbinger of spring as they leaf out two weeks earlier than anything else in the wild. Also, the brilliant crimson and orange fall colours are the brightest of any of our native plants. These are thorny, so transplanting and handling can be made easier by cutting them back severely before digging. With a good root ball, the new growth quickly replaces what has been removed at the time of digging.

Russet buffaloberry: a tough shrub which can survive in sun or shade in almost any type of soil, it is easily identified by the rusty colour on the underside of the leaf. Female specimens produce clumps of red berries along the stem. Follow the instructions for digging gooseberry, and again, do not be hesitant to prune these back at the time of digging for better results later on.

Red twig dogwood: the bright red bark stands out best after the ground warms, and before other plants leaf out. Another desirable ornamental quality is the subtle purplish-red fall colour which lingers after most other plants have dropped their leaves. One can either dig a single small specimen or, on an older bush, find a lower branch or "stolon" that has drooped onto the soil surface and rooted itself. Cut the stolon away from the parent plant, then clip away all the remaining growth above the first or second leaf scar. Once re-established, cut the old wood out as it loses its colour.

Potentilla: this yellow-flowering shrub is both drought resistant and frost resistant. Its tidy shape rarely needs pruning. Dig bare root using a bucket of water and prune back hard. Potentilla is effective in almost any part of the garden which requires a cheerful accent. As it is rather drab in winter it's a good idea to plant with evergreen material nearby. Unlike the commercial hybrids, the native variety has unique grey-green leaves.

Many gardeners avoid transplanting some types of native shrubs, such as wild rose or buckbrush which thrive so well under cultivation that they can become invasive. Such species spread with very deep roots and are therefore difficult to contain. Gardeners who wish to incorporate such material into their landscapes are advised to treat them like mint, surrounded by an extremely deep edging, or to confine them to background areas where they can spread freely without interference.

Common juniper: the only evergreen native to the foothills which can be considered as a shrub, though it rarely grows above knee-high. This one is very prickly to the touch. When growing in shade and shelter, it has a grass green colour and an open, fern-like shape. In exposed sunny areas it becomes more compact and tends to be olive or golden green in colour.

It is difficult to transplant any specimen larger than a dinner plate. Try to find seedlings in clay soil on a bank or cut where a parent plant higher up has dropped berries below. In the garden landscape, planting this species is a good way to maintain a bank because once it matures and spreads it will discourage most weeds and grasses that try to grow under it.

Native Ground Covers:
There are three evergreen ground covers which make an excellent addition to any landscape. In terms of beauty and hardiness they are equal if not better than some of the imported species which are sold commercially.

Horizontal juniper: This one is not prickly and mature specimens make large carpets only a few centimetres high. The colour can vary from blue to blue-green in summer though they all turn a beautiful mauve shade for a few weeks in fall. Winter colour can be anything from murky brown, to rusty orange to navy blue or gray.

The most successfully transplanted specimens are the smallest ones, found in the same sorts of spots as the common juniper previously cited. A young plant will send out one "branch" in one direction along the ground. If the branch is about arm's length and the stem no thicker than a pencil, cut it back to about 6 inches or 10 centimeters, then try to obtain enough root ball to fill a one gallon bucket.

On mature specimens the creeping branches often root themselves. If there appears to be a strong bundle of hair roots near the tip of a young and healthy stem or branch, it can be transplanted just like the stolon on a dogwood, by cutting it away from the parent plant and tipping it back towards the root bundle.

Kinnikinick or bearberry: is the only woody, broad-leafed evergreen native to the northern sector of the chinook zone. Under cultivation, it makes great masses of delicate pink flowers in June which produce red berries in late summer. It seems to thrive equally well in full sun or partial shade.

Guidelines to locating this species, its growth habit and transplanting techniques are exactly the same as for the horizontal juniper. These two often grow side by side and are outstanding fall and winter accents. A picture of the two growing intertwined introduces the chapter on ground covers. They can be used effectively to cascade down a bank or over the lip of a planter.

Both species can now also be purchased in commercial garden centres as potted specimens. The Latin name for Kinnikinick is *Arctostaphylos uva-ursi*. A variety of horizontal juniper sold under the name of "Prince of Wales", refers to a plant selected at the Duke of Windsor's old ranch near Pekisko, where it grows in abundance.

Wintergreen (pyrola): is an evergreen perennial which grows among the leaf mould in forested areas of the chinook zone. It is not yet sold comcercially. The flower stalk and round leaves are like a miniature version of the imported bergenia, and they act exactly the same. That is, in winter the leaves hug the ground whenever the temperature drops below freezing, but stand up brightly whenever it thaws.

Wintergreen grows in among so many other grasses and perennials that it is best to move them bare root. Since they are among the first to break dormancy, they should be dug as soon as possible after the ground thaws. Remove a clod of earth with a sharp trowel or shovel. In the shade of your body and out of the wind, carefully but quickly remove excess soil and other plant material until you are left with only the white, interconnected root system. Wrap in wet burlap and keep them damp, cool and shaded until replanting. Or, if you can carry a bucket of water to where these are dug, immerse the clod of earth and gently swirl it around until the soil and other plant material falls away. If these are left in the bucket for more than a couple of days before planting, they will rot.

As an evergreen, wintergreen performs best when planted in conditions similar to where it is found growing wild; that is, rich soil in shelter and partial shade.

There are a couple of other native perennials which merit trial in the garden. The wild strawberry can be used as a ground cover, and the wild geranium in the perennial bed. Both are what could be termed semi-evergreen, but how long the leaves persist and how fresh they look in spring will depend on where they've been planted and the amount of snow cover received in a particular winter. In a rigorous, sunny location during a relatively snowless winter, the leaves are apt to shrivel up and blow away. In sheltered or shady parts of the garden where snow lingers longest, these will perform like evergreens, but then one is not apt to get a lot of berries or flowers in summer if there is too little sun.

Transplanting From Other Areas

We have a number of different microclimates within the foothills chinook zone which range from dry, exposed hilltops to damp, frosty bottomland. You may transplant from nearby but different horticultural zones if you wish to find plant material for a particular area in your garden. For example: if you wish to find plant material for a hot dry area such as a south-facing bed under the eaves of your home, drive to one of the desert zones to find suitable transplants. Without crossing west of the continental divide, there is a wealth of different but adaptable plant material in areas which are within easy driving distance of our high altitude zone.

Plants from the Semi-Desert Zone:

From almost any part of the foothills chinook zone one can drive east to find plants that are well-suited to the driest, hottest parts of the garden. To avoid introducing other undesirable grasses or perennials into the garden, it is often best to move the following bare root, using a bucket or wet burlap, as with wintergreen.

Sagebrush: has only recently been found to serve as a useful ornamental. Though it often looks scraggly in the wild, it bushes out nicely in a tended area and is easily shaped if desired. Some specimens will grow waist high in a sheltered spot. Though the leaves dry out in winter, they do persist and retain a beautiful silver-blue sheen which stands out best against a dark background like rocks, earth-toned siding or a planting of common juniper. The flower stalks are not particularly showy and tend to flop all over, so it is better to trim them off as they form on the plant.

Sagebrush breaks dormancy and leafs out very early, so it should be transplanted in late March or early April if the season allows. Cut back the branches as with gooseberry.

Prickly-pear Cactus: makes a good ground cover for that hot, dry spot under the eaves on the south side of the house. It flowers more profusely and will grow taller under cultivation than in the wild. Makes a good background for cactus-like annuals such as portulaca, zinnias or Livingstone Daisy.

Hawthorn: shows up in gullies and river valleys throughout the semi-desert zone. Its growth habit (small tree or large shrub) and adaptability to extremely rigorous conditions makes it an excellent substitute for caragana.

Silver-leafed Buffaloberry: is one of the few native shrubs now being sold commercially, but it is easily transplanted from gullies and ditches in the semi-desert zone. The thorns are like those of hawthorn, but the leaves resemble wolf willow at a distance. The tart berries are showy and make good jam.

Plants from the Boreal Forest Zone:

Plants from this zone are well adapted to heavy soils and the extremely short growing season which occurs in the most westerly part of our own zone. The boreal forest meets the alpine part of the chinook zone about 50 miles (80 kilometres) north-west of Calgary. Many of the plants also follow the Red Deer River Valley down towards Drumheller. The following two are worth collecting:

Tamarack or larch: is our only native deciduous conifer. These take on a very broad, but pointed conical shape and should be set no closer than 15 feet (5 metres) from other trees and shrubs. Not a good tree for the small urban garden, but great for the farm or acreage where it can be back-planted with evergreens to bring out the golden fall colour.

White Birch: looks best when planted in a clump or encouraged to grow with several stems just as it does in the wild. On exposed sites these make good accent trees, but are disappointingly slow growing. They will do much better in the cool, sheltered valleys of our zone, but should never be planted where they are expected to create shelter or attain great size.

Plants from the Central and Southern Chinook Zone:

It is because the Rockies and foothills get increasingly higher as we go southward that many plants such as Colorado blue spruce have been brought northward with great success. Some lesser known things work just as well:

Ponderosa pine: turns up near the international border in the Waterton area. It has extremely long needles and the orangey-red bark on older specimens makes it a good ornamental. It is long-lived, and requires as much space as tamarac. Look for seedlings about knee-high or shorter. The roots are very sensitive to drying so they must be dug and put in a bucket of water or wet burlap almost instantly. The same precautions apply when planting. They should never be moved once the buds have swelled, so timing is the same as for sagebrush.

Creeping mahonia: is an evergreen ground cover with large, holly-like leaves which turn brilliant shades of orange, red and purple in fall. The transplanting technique and the best planting location is the same as for wintergreen.

Huckleberry: is another evergreen ground cover which resembles kinnikinick except that the leaves are softer and more pointed. Transplanting is the same as for kinnikinick. After a snowless winter, the ones growing in partial shade seem to look best.

Roses
by Anne Vale

Anyone who says you can't grow roses in Alberta should go and take a look at the University of Alberta Botanic Garden at Devon, or the rose garden at the Alberta Horticultural Research Centre at Brooks.

At Devon they run a varietal trial where more than sixty shrub rose cultivars are grown, and tested for hardiness in Alberta. At Brooks, the rose garden has been established for many years and there are mature samples of all roses which are hardy in Alberta and also a large number of the hardier hybrid teas and floribundas. The best time to visit these places to see the roses in bloom is the end of June. Although neither location receives the extreme chinooks that we get south of Calgary along the foothills, they are the closest demonstration gardens available to us. They provide a very good hardiness guide, and most of the roses which do well for them will grow here.

Hardy Shrub Roses

These are the ones which need no winter protection here and very little pruning. They mature into big vigourous bushes which fit in well with an informal country setting. They bear very little resemblance to the neat formal roses known as hybrid teas. Shrub roses usually flower for a short burst at the end of June and beginning of July with a profusion of bloom. Their perfume scents the whole garden. Most have ornamental rose hips which stay on the bush all winter and look good against the snow. This type of rose is very trouble free. It is happy with our conditions, doesn't mind the chinooks, and needs very little pruning because it blooms best on the older wood. Varieties usually are listed in catalogues under Hardy Shrub Roses but may sometimes be listed under Rugosa Roses. Many are the same varieties that have been grown in English cottage gardens for generations and some were grown by Napoleon's Josephine in France. Empress Josephine was bent on making her gardens the finest in Europe and collected every known variety of rose numbering about 250 different ones. Her official artist was Pierre-Joseph Redoute, whose rose paintings still appear on calendars, table mats and flower prints in every department store today. Most of today's shrub roses are descended from these roses of the early 1800's. Others have been bred right here in Alberta using the hardiest shrub roses and throwing in a dash of our native rose for good measure. Mr. Georges Bugnet (pronounced boon yay) of Legal, Alberta, has produced a hybrid "Therese Bugnet" which is a delightful double pink rose, with continuous bloom all summer. It grows to a height of six feet.

Other well known shrub roses of great hardiness have been introduced by the Agriculture Research Station at Morden, Manitoba, among them "Cuthbert Grant", "Prairie Dawn", "Adelaide Hoodless', and "Metis", "Hansa", and "Persian Yellow".

Hardy Hybrid Shrub Roses

Reds:
Adelaide Hoodless
Height: 3 feet

Introduced by Henry Marshall at Morden Research Station, Manitoba. Semi-double red flowers in clusters of up to 25. Slightly fragrant. Blooms all summer.

Cuthbert Grant
Height: 3 feet

Another one of Henry Marshall's. Dark red double blooms like a hybrid tea. Blooms all summer. A real beauty.

Hansa
Height: 5 feet

A Rugosa hybrid. Magenta-red, double, fragrant. Blooms freely all season. Very tough.

F.J. Grootendorst
Height: 6 feet

A Rugosa hybrid. Small double flowers borne in clusters, bright red petals with fringed edges. Blooms early summer.

Grootendorst Supreme
Height: 6 feet

Like "F.J. Grootendorst", but crimson.

Magnifica
Height: 4 feet

Semi-double red. Blooms July and August providing you keep old blossoms picked off.

Yellows:
Agnes
Height: 6 feet

A Canadian rose from Ottawa. Very hardy. Amber yellow double blooms, very fragrant. Blooms early summer.

Persian Yellow

Height: 6 feet

Deep yellow double blooms on the older wood in early summer. A tall vigourous bush. May be trained as a rambler.

Harrisons Yellow

Height: 6 feet

Very similar to Persian Yellow, a cross between the Austrian Brier and Scotch Brier, brought with the early settlers - has thrived all over Canada ever since.

Austrian Copper

Height: 6 feet

A single flame orange bloom, closely related to the Persian Yellow. Blooms in early summer.

Whites:

Blanc Double de Coubert

Height: 5 feet

A Rugosa hybrid. Flowers are semi-double, white and fragrant.

Sir Thomas Lipton

Height: 2 feet

A delightful white double rose, closely resembling a hybrid tea. Small spreading bush, very fragrant.

Altaica

This cultivar of the Scotch Rose is one of the hardiest. Single white flowers, followed by round black hips.

Pinks:

Prairie Dawn

Height: 6 feet

Introduced by Morden Research Station, Manitoba. Double shell-pink flowers, fragrant. Hardy and vigourous. Blooms continuously all summer.

Therese Bugnet

Height: 6 feet

Developed in Alberta. Blooms on the old wood from June till frost. Double pink, fragrant.

Pink Grootendorst

Height: 5 feet

Clusters of small shell pink fringed blooms in June and again in August. A Rugosa hybrid.

Betty Bland

Height: 6 feet

Bred from one of Canada's native roses, Betty Bland is very hardy. A semi-double pink rose with smooth red stems. Blooms in July.

Red Leaf Rose
Height: 5-6 feet
This rose is grown more for the landscape value of its red leaves and red hips than its flowers which are single pink blooms like the wild rose.

This list of hardy hybrid shrub roses contains only those roses which are easily available and proven hardy. There are many others which are worth a try if you can find them under the heading of Shrub Roses or Rugosa Roses. More are constantly being developed and new varieties being placed on the market. The current edition of Alberta Horticulture Guide will keep you up to date.

Tender Roses
Hybrid tea roses can be grown here but require much special care and winter protection. Their blooms do not reach the size and magnificence that they achieve in more temperate climates. Our Alberta air seems to suck the moisture out of them and in most cases they are disappointing and short lived. However, Eileen Jameson recommends the following methods for protecting tender roses in winter.
Method One: Hill up the soil around each plant and cover with paper cones.
Method Two: Trim rose to fit a large cardboard box, fertilize and soak, then place a cardboard box over the rose with the flaps open at both ends and fill with peat moss. The lower flaps are covered with soil, and the upper flaps are left open until the ground is frozen. Then they are closed in and another box is placed over the top to prevent the melting snow from running through and dampening the peat moss. This method has enabled us to save Queen Elizabeth and Peace roses for twelve to sixteen years.

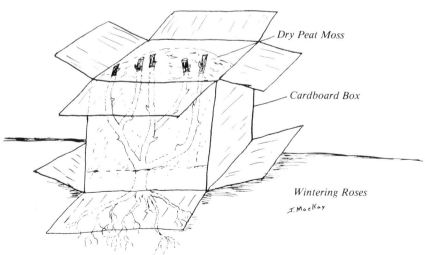

Dry Peat Moss

Cardboard Box

Wintering Roses
J. MacKay

When purchasing hybrid tea roses which you intend to keep over the winter you should be careful to order only those which have Rosa Canina as a rootstock. Catalogues which supply the prairies should state this loud and clear. Beware of falling for glossy pictures in some eastern catalogues. These hybrid teas will not winter here. Certain cultivars are hardier than others however, and provided they are on R. Canina rootstock, they should be worth a trial given suitable winter protection.

Mr. Lincoln

Rich, fragrant, dark velvety red. Fully double five to six inch blooms which last well.

Crimson Glory

Very similar to "Mr. Lincoln" above.

Peace

Creamy yellow with pink edges. One of the hardiest hybrid teas. Tall vigourous disease resistant bush.

Queen Elizabeth

Makes a very tall strong bush, clusters of huge double pink flowers on strong stems. Fragrant.

Peace Redgold

Golden yellow buds become less yellow as flowers open and the red continues to suffuse the bloom - very lovely.

Centurio

A dark velvety red, fragrant and prolific.

Peer Gynt

Large golden yellow, abundant blooms, very fragrant.

Tropicana

Perfectly shaped, orange-red fragrant. Very prolific.

Woburn Abbey

Apricot orange blooms.

Virgo

One of the best whites, fragrant and abundant.

Miniature Roses

These are seldom hardy over the winter and are best taken in to the basement or greenhouse over the cold weather and grown in pots. Many colours and varieties are available. They are very susceptible to spider mites.

Climbing Roses

Unfortunately there is as yet no climbing rose which is hardy in Alberta. They bloom on the year-old wood and they are too tender to survive the winter so that the canes put up the first year are dead by the next year when they are supposed to bloom. If you have one you may try burying the canes totally in fall, but they are usually a disappointment.

Planting of Roses

A. Packaged roses, with bare roots, should be removed from the packaging as soon as received and soaked in a tank of water so that the whole plant is completely submerged for twenty-four hours. Roses have very deep roots and the planting area should be prepared to a depth of at least 12" - preferably deeper. Dig a hole at least 18" deep and a foot across and mix a handful of bone meal with the loose soil in the bottom of the hole. Spread the roots out in the hole and fill in around them with good soil so that the graft is buried two inches deep. Water deeply. Then pile loose soil up around the branches till the whole plant is completely buried. Leave this extra covering on for two weeks until the plant has begun to bud, at which time you may carefully remove the top insulating layer by hand.

B. Provided they are in containers which will disintegrate, roses should be planted intact in their pots so that their roots are not disturbed. Make sure the afore-mentioned procedure is followed as regards digging the hole, but you do not need to hill up around the plant for the first two weeks.

Fertilizing of Roses

Roses are heavy feeders and like lots of fertilizer. Large quantities of bone meal and surface applications of well-rotted manure are appreciated. Commercial rose food may be used as directed on the packet and a mulch of grass clippings, peat moss or bark chips will help prevent dehydration in hot weather.

Pruning of Roses

a. Hybrid Teas: Do not prune in fall or winter. Wait until early May to prune. If more blooms are the aim, do not prune too severely; but if exhibition flowers are what you want, cut the branches back to about 4" to 6" in length. This will give you fewer but bigger blooms. Remove any dead wood entirely and cut live branches back to an outfacing bud.

b. Shrub Roses: These bloom on the older wood and do not need much pruning except to remove any dead wood and any very old unproductive branches from the base of the bush.

Both shrub roses and hybrid teas occasionally produce suckers. These need to be removed. Suckers are vigourous shoots which appear from below where the union was made with the cultivated rose and the root stock. The sucker will be the same type of rose as was used for the rootstock, usually Rosa Canina. They will be quite different in appearance from the cultivated variety of the bush: usually thorny, tall, and with 3 or more pairs of leaves as opposed to the rest of the bush which usually has only two pairs of leaves. These suckers should be removed from below ground level. Scrape dirt away until you can cut off the sucker where it grows from the root. They will not bloom and just sap the energy from the rose you are trying to cultivate.

Don't confuse suckers with offshoots which may spring from roses grown on their own roots. These will be identical to their parent plant and are a good method of propagating your rose bush.

Storing Trees and Shrubs Over Winter
by Norma Lyall

What do you do with those pots of trees and shrubs that you didn't get planted in time? In 1979 I had about thirty pots - some were spruce, there was an apple tree, northwest poplar, sharp leaf willow and two flats of little pansies which I dug out of the garden to transplant but never did. Our problem was what to do with all these plants - let them die or what.

One day I said, "Couldn't we put all these pots in this big pile of old wood shavings which we had stock piled for further use?" So we hauled all the pots to the shavings pile and we started to set the pots tight together down in the shavings. We dug them in the full depth of the pots plus four inches on top of the pots with the tree or shrub sticking out above the shavings. The flats of pansies were put a foot deep in the shavings.

This was a success - everything survived. One or two of the pansies were in bloom and looked the same when we dug them out of the shavings in spring. There was no trouble with mice as the shavings were wet.

 **Helpful Hints**

When planting trees and shrubs put a small shovelful of oats or barley in the bottom of the hole. The fermentation of the grain causes heat which helps roots to form. Avoid heavy use of fertilizer - either manure or chemical fertilizer - at the time of planting as it burns tiny roots which are essential to the survival of the tree or shrub.

Water trees and shrubs well in late fall to prevent dehydration in winter. Spray anti-desiccant on trees on a warm day in late fall to protect from drying winds. Mulch after freeze up.

When planting hybrid tea roses in spring - plant early according to directions but hill them right over with loose soil. Leave it on for two weeks and then remove carefully by hand.

Junipers love lime so sprinkle wood ashes around the base of them.

For anything that loves acid, such as larch trees, put rhubarb leaves and stalks around the base of the plants.

Chapter Five

Propagation
and Shelterbelts

Seed Propagation of Woody Perennials
by Pam and Ken Wright

The most probable deterrent to propagation of woody perennials by seed is the time involved to get a tree or shrub of noticeable size from a seed. This shouldn't be so; after all, many yards are dotted with seedlings of Manitoba Maple (Box Elder), Green Ash, some elms, poplars, lilacs, even a few conifers, to name a few plants that shed their seeds rather freely.

Every year many people plant vegetable and flower seeds quite successfully. This success can be matched with woody perennials (trees and shrubs), with a few extra steps. Some steps are the same as those taken by the ambitious gardener who saves the seed from the most outstanding vegetable or flower, to replant the following years.

Seed selection is the first step - any hardy and usually locally grown plant will make a good seed source. Take time to check the form of the plant, the colour of blossoms, leaf colour, flavour of fruit (as with choke-cherry, elderberry, and other edibles). Look to see if the plant has been attacked by insects as some cultivars are more susceptible than others. Stay away from apples and named fruit trees. They are hybrids and do not breed true from seed, although if the plants are proven hardy, they do make good windbreak or shelter-belt trees, but you won't get a Goodland apple from a Goodland apple seed.

Collecting seeds must by done at the right time, that is to say, before they are gone; taken by birds, animals, wind or gravity. Cones can be

---

On Facing Page
Top: Garden shelterbelt.
Centre: Semi-mature hedge rows enhance a typical foothills farmstead.
Bottom: Trees break the wind, rocks hold heat.

59

plucked right from the tree before they are fully ripened, then dried and shaken to dislodge the seeds. Sometimes a rodent's cache can be found where cones are plentiful and ready for the taking. Dry seeds, such as lilacs or green ash are easily collected by picking directly off the plant, or spreading a sheet under the tree or shrub, then shaking the plant to dislodge the seeds. Break off any woody material that remains attached to the seeds. Fleshy fruits such as saskatoon, mountain ash, Nanking cherry, plums, chokecherry, elderberry, etc., must be taken from the plants before they start to dry, and cleaned to remove all fleshy material. This is easily done by breaking the skin by hand, then running water over all in a sieve, or similar utensil, to wash away the pulp, and placing on a paper or screen to dry. All seeds should be stored in paper bags or boxes, in a cool, dry, dark place, the same way you store vegetable seeds.

Woody perennial seeds, as a rule, have to undergo a stratification, or moist chilling period in order to break dormancy. There are 4 factors involved in this: moisture, aeration, time and temperature.

Moist peat moss is an excellent medium for seed stratification. Peat moss should be thoroughly mixed with water, wet to the point of almost dripping when a handful is squeezed. If it drips it is too wet. If it is too dry insufficient moisture is absorbed by the seed coat, too wet and mold problems arise. Mix seeds with 2 to 3 times as much peat as seed. Seal in plastic bags, which allow air exchange; the reason, plastic works as a mulch. Then label accordingly and store in the root cellar or refrigerator, optimum temperature 2°C - 7°C, for 60 - 90 days.

Seeds stratified in January or so are ready for planting in the spring. Sow your seeds outside in beds prepared the same way you would prepare beds for vegetables; uniform soil mixture, raked smooth, etc. The rules for seeding woody perennials are the same as for vegetables. Don't plant seeds deeper than 3 times the diameter of the seed. Keep moist during germination as dry soil interferes with oxygen exchange. Keep those weeds under control. Allow for the fact that several years may pass before you move your seedlings.

This spring and summer watch for the trees and/or shrubs that you would like to propagate. When the fruit matures, pick your seeds, just before the birds do.

One last note, please label all of your seeds as to date, place and kind picked, and time stratified.

Propagation by Cuttings
by Pam and Ken Wright

Propagation by cuttings is a very advantageous practice because the characteristics of the new plant are generally the same as the parent plant. There are several types of cuttings, and the plant to be propagated usually dictates the method to be used.

1. Root cuttings - red raspberry, aspen *(Populus tremuloides)*
2. Stem cuttings -
    a) from a soft new wood - poplar, rose, willow, lilac
    b) from a hard older wood - spirea, rose, willow, poplar, currant, some conifers
    c) semi-hardwood - junipers, conifers, aspen, arbor-vitae

The first step in propagating woody perennials (trees and shrubs) by stem cutting is to select the plant to be used for a cutting source, taking into consideration the characteristics of the plant, susceptibility to disease or insects, environment, and amount of cutting material, which is the newest growth. Cuttings at least 3 inches long, 6-8 inches being preferable, should be cut cleanly with sharp pruning clippers or shears that have been cleaned with household bleach. Cuttings root more easily when the cut is made directly below a bud, having 3 or more buds on the length.

Suitable rooting mediums are:
    a) sawdust (not cedar) - is easily accessible, easy to keep wet, and is easy to move when the cuttings have rooted
    b) sand - retains a lot of moisture, but not much air exchange
    c) Jiffy-7's - are fine for smaller cuttings of soft-wood if they can be kept constantly moist
    d) perlite - is also very hard to keep moist, but works well for juniper semi-hardwood cuttings
    e) the ground - a fine medium for hard-wood cuttings of easily rooting plants such as poplar and willow

The Art of Propagating a Shelter Belt
by Art L. Patterson

If you have longed to have a windbreak of hardy poplar trees glistening in the summer breeze, then start today and plan for one. A shelter-belt, envied and admired by all who see it, is a sight you will be proud of. The method I am about to describe to you will cost very little, as far as the cost of cuttings are concerned. The labour entailed in achieving this delightful windbreak can be charged to the labour of love. Without the initiative, the enthusiasm, and a constant effort in the care of these trees, things just don't happen; so be prepared to carry through from start to finish, if you are to achieve the desired effect.

Method: Consider, visualize, and anticipate your dream of a windbreak as you would like to have it; taking into account the prevailing winds, the factors of drainage which may be used to your advantage, and the soil conditions. Obstacles which sometimes present a problem have to be considered, since no one plan will fit all circumstances.

Having considered these factors, then make a start by preparing the land for planting. It is advisable to summer fallow a strip for 2 years, wide enough to accommodate the anticipated windbreak, bearing in mind that these little cuttings 6-8 inches long will soon be stately trees up to 30 feet tall. When planning the windbreak strip always bear in mind that trees must have room to grow and as they grow must have cultivation, so leave 16-20 feet between rows so you will be able to cultivate between with a tractor. They will need to be cultivated on both sides for 3 years and on the outsides for the next 4 years.

An ideal windbreak for this country would be a strip wide enough to accommodate a row of non-suckering caraganas on the outside, which are tough and will protect the poplars until they get started. Then 2 rows of Northwest, Brooks, or Russian Poplars for fast growth and something to watch while a row of spruce trees, which are long-lasting, but slower in growth, get established in the front row.

Cuttings and rooted trees can be obtained free by contacting your District Agriculturalist, providing that the land preparation requirements have been met; or you can take your own cuttings from cultivated poplar trees in your vicinity. Stay away from native varieties, eg. trembling aspen (white poplar).

When selecting cuttings, be sure to take them from male trees, as these trees are not fluff-bearing. It has been found that the female species of poplar are very beautiful trees, but they produce the seed fluff in the spring. (The female is always making a fuzz about something!) You can determine which are the male trees by observation in the spring. Male trees drop their catkins about 3 weeks before the females let go their fluff.

Cuttings should be 6-8 inches, taken from last year's growth which is limber, and has buds appearing on the surface. A good cutting has 3 or 4 buds, is 6-8 inches long, has the bottom cut at an angle, and the top cut square off. One branch can give you several cuttings. Use a sharp hand pruner. Take these cuttings in March or before the sap starts to flow, and wrap them in burlap in bundles of 25 or so. Place them in a cool damp place, away from frost, always putting the tops or square cuts up. This will keep the cuttings dormant until planting.

The cuttings we used to plant our windbreak came from Indian Head, Saskatchewan. They arrived in the spring, and to say the least they looked very small and insignificant.

Having never planted cuttings, I was a little skeptical, but we planted them just the same and were delighted with the result. Not more than 10 out of the 1000 we planted died. I was so pleased and delighted with the end result, that I have been looking at them and talking about them ever since.

The method of planting these cuttings is important and holds some hints that are useful. This is what we did!

Steps to Take:
1. The land is prepared and ready to grow.

2. The cuttings are at hand.
3. The time to plant is in the spring when the land is warm, the leaves are just bursting on the trees, and all things in nature have the urge to grow.
4. Establish the location of the row to be. Stake it out leaving 18-20 feet between rows, and 14-16 feet between each set.
5. Take one or two bundles of cuttings from storage and place them in a bucket which has a little water in it. This saves the cuttings from drying out while you plant.
6. Take one cutting and push it into the moist summer fallow on an angle of 60^0, pointing to the southeast. Only one bud should appear above the ground on the top side of the cutting, and this bud is at ground level. Place a second cutting about 10-12 inches away from the first cutting. This establishes a set, thereby doubling your chances of ending up with one good tree in each spot. Planting the cutting at an angle enables you to pack the soil around it more firmly. The tighter it is packed, the sooner it begins to take root. The reason we place the cutting facing southeast is to expose the least amount of bark to the direct sunlight, and encourage the bud to grow straight up.
7. The following spring, remove the weaker tree from each set.

Our experience has shown that for shelter belts, cuttings are much preferable to rooted trees, because they don't need watering. Each cutting only puts up as much growth as its root system can support.

Our shelter belt was planted 20 years ago, using this method. In 5 years, with no supplementary watering, the trees were 12 to 15 feet high! They are now about 30 feet tall, with 12 inch trunks.

 **Helpful Hints**

Use canisters from 35mm film to save your seeds as they are airtight.

Chapter Six

Lawns and Groundcovers

Lawns
by Bill Jackson

There is without a doubt satisfaction in having a green healthy lawn that is free of disease and weeds. However, each has to decide for himself how important the lawn is and how much time he wishes to spend on it in comparison to the rest of the yard and garden.

There are some basic things that will help you to have a good lawn without too much effort.

The first thing is to choose the proper seed mixture for your location. If your lawn can be watered and is in a sunny location I recommend 25% Kentucky Bluegrass, 75% Creeping Red Fescue, or if the lawn is in a shady location use 100% Creeping Red Fescue. If there is not going to be supplementary water available then seed 100% Crested Wheat Grass.

In Alberta, June seems to be the best month for starting lawns, although lawns have been planted from May to September. Success has also been achieved by seeding in October just before freeze up.

Some form of raking the lawn in spring is beneficial as it helps to aerate the lawn which assists the grass roots to breathe.

The moisture requirements of established lawns will depend on two factors; the soil on which the grass is growing and the rate of moisture loss from the turf itself. If there is insufficient rain and you are going to water the lawn, be sure to give it 1½" or more of moisture. Light waterings do more harm than good as they encourage a shallow root system.

On Facing Page
Top: A weed-free lawn emphasizes plantings.
Centre left: Snow-in-summer is a fast filler while slower growing Juniper takes over.
Centre right: Easily grown goutweed thrives in shade.
Bottom: Native evergreens, kinnikinnick with red berries and horizontal juniper with blue berries.

Your lawn will benefit from a spring fertilizing with 27-14-0 or 16-20-0 at the rate of five pounds per 1000 square feet. Be sure it is spread evenly. Apply to a dry lawn and then water in well. You can repeat the process in early July. Do not fertilize late in the growing season, although some people do so in late October in readiness for spring. This is a practice I haven't used as I feel that more benefits are derived from the fertilizer if it is applied in spring.

A well-established and well-managed lawn is rarely subject to severe weed problems. It is better to try and build up the condition of the lawn than to apply herbicides. However, if you choose to use herbicides, they are best applied in summer when there are optimum temperatures and usually fewer windy days. Follow directions carefully.

Regular mowing at frequent intervals is required to maintain a good turf. When maintained at a height of 1½ to 2" lawn grasses will compete favourably with weeds.

The most devastating turf disease is snow mould, caused by a fungus that is active only during the winter season. We have an area on our lawn where the snow is slow to melt that is prone to snow mould. I have found that by removing snow from this shady area to speed up melting there is no longer a problem with this disease.

Another disease common to lawns is fairy rings, which are caused by a mushroom fungus which if allowed to develop will cause circular or sometimes crescent shaped patches of dead turf. The infected areas increase in size progressively from the center and in the early stages show up as bright green rings. Later the turf inside the rings becomes thin, turns yellow and eventually dies out. Recommended control measures involve punching 6" deep holes through the turf, applying 11-48-0 fertilizer and spraying with an organic wetting agent. Water heavily at the rate of 2 to 3" per week and continue to water heavily every 1 or 2 days for 3 to 4 weeks. This procedure may need to be repeated for several years to completely rid the lawn of fairy rings. An alternate method would be to dig out and remove the infected area, replace with fresh soil and reseed.

A healthy, well-kept lawn adds greatly to the beauty of a house and garden, and is actually not too hard to achieve. If you would like more details about lawns, Alberta Agriculture has a publication entitled "Lawn Building and Maintenance" that is available from your local district agriculturalist.

Ground Covers
by Anne Vale

Ground cover is the term used to describe any plant which will spread to form a solid mat over the ground.

They are useful where mowing is difficult, such as on a steep bank, under a tree or around a rock. They can also be used in bold sweeping patches to reduce the amount of mowing necessary or to fill in an awkward space. They may be combined with larger plants, boulders or driftwood as a focal point. Once established they require minimum care and can be an attractive addition to your landscape.

It is very important to prepare the site properly. The ground should be cultivated and raked smooth and cleaned of all weeds. It is best to first prepare the area intended for ground cover plants and let it lie fallow the first year so that you may control any weeds with a systemic weed killer of a type which will not persist in the soil. If your ground cover area borders a lawn it will be necessary to provide a barrier to prevent the grass roots creeping into the ground cover or vice versa. A border of 2''x6'' treated lumber set on edge flush with the ground will do the job. Various types of edging are on the market today. We recommend the 6'' width. The appearance of these may be disguised with the clever use of rocks or bricks.

Ground cover plants will not win the battle with existing weeds but given a clean bed and good well-prepared soil they will grow so closely together that after the first couple of years no new weed will be able to get a foothold. Therefore it is most important to start with clean soil and keep it weeded until your young ground cover plants have become firmly established.

Suitable plants vary from shrubby material such as juniper, kinnikinnick, yellow clematis or pachistima to succulents like hen and chickens or stonecrop and even strawberries. Some spread further and faster than others and you should determine their mature spread and plant them a little closer than their ultimate expected spread, so that they mesh closely together and form a dense mat. Stonecrop will spread a long way in one year and so will goutweed but others which are very attractive as ground covers are not so invasive and will need closer planting to be effective within 2 years.

To cover a large area with bought plants can be very expensive but a lot can be accomplished with seed, or by starting your own slips in a nursery bed the first year while you are waiting for your ground to be free of weeds.

Most of the ground cover plants will not like being walked on but you can solve the problem by the clever use of stepping stones to make a path, or with a prickly bush to stop people cutting a corner, etc. There are plants to suit a wide variety of situations in sun or shade, light or heavy soils, dry or damp locations.

Ground Covers

Plant	Propagation	Soil and Moisture	Sun or Shade	Distance Apart
Arctic Phlox *(Phlox borealis)*	division	sandy well drained	sun	12"
Bugleweed (Ajuga)	division	heavy moist	shade	8"
Clematis Tangutica (yellow)	seed	sandy well drained	sun	3'
Cliff Green (Pachistima)	division	any well drained	either	12"
Creeping Jenny *(Lysimachia nummularia)*	division	heavy moist	sun	18"
Goutweed or Snow-on-the-Mountain *(Aegopodium podagraria)*	division	heavy moist	shade	18"
Hen and Chickens (several kinds)	division	any well drained	sun	12"
Japanese Spurge *(Pachysandra terminalis)*	division	any well drained acid soil	shade	12"
Juniper, most spreading types	cuttings or layering	any well drained	either	3'-4'
Kinnikinnick	cuttings or layering	any well drained	either	12"
Lily of the Valley	division	heavy moist	shade	18"
Maiden Pinks *(Dianthus deltoides)*	seed or division	sandy well drained	sun	12"
Moss Phlox *(Phlox subulata)*	division	sandy well drained	sun	12"
Periwinkle *(Vinca minor)*	cuttings	any well drained	shade	18"
Sedum (several kinds)	division	any well drained	sun	18"
Snow-in-Summer *(Cerastium tomentosum)*	seed or division	any well drained	sun	18"
Strawberry	runners	heavy moist	sun	18"
Thyme	seed or division	any well drained	sun	18"
Virginia Creeper *(Parthenocissus quinquefolia)*	cuttings	heavy moist	either	3'

 **Helpful Hints**

Female dogs urinating on the lawn can cause burn spots. Train them to use the driveway. To minimize damage to lawns water thoroughly to dilute the urine.

To keep grass from growing between bricks in a walk, sprinkle the spaces with salt or pour salted boiling water on grass or weeds.

To get rid of thistles wait until after a good rain storm and then pull them — usually you can get the whole root. Or, cut them and put an eyedropper of fuel oil down the hollow stem.

Chapter Seven

Annual Flowers

Many members of the Millarville Horticultural Club start a number of their annual flower seeds indoors which enables them to grow a larger variety of annual flowers as well as to have annuals blooming earlier than if they were sown directly into their gardens.

Seed sowing indoors or in the greenhouse is easy. Both methods follow the same set of rules. The greenhouse provides ideal conditions but the windowsill method has to be adapted to survive the excess heat and lack of light encountered in the average home. Supplementary light in the form of fluorescent lamps is a great help to indoor growing. These should be no less than 6'' from the tops of the seedlings and should not be turned on for more than 18 hours a day.

For beginner growers trying the indoor method it is advisable to stick with the things which need only a short period to grow to transplanting size such as marigolds, asters, alyssum, cabbage, tomatoes, etc.

You may use any shallow container with good drainage holes, but best results are obtained in a wooden flat with slats allowing good drainage from below. You may easily make your own small flat from a lath, a hammer and a few shingle nails. Leave about ¼'' space between the slats on the bottom of your flat.

Soil Mixture for Starting Seeds:
>2 parts loam put through ¼" wire mesh screen to
>remove stones, sticks and lumps of clay
>1 part peat moss soaked in hot water
>½ part of fine vermiculite

Add vermiculite to wet peat moss and then mix with loam. Put this damp mixture in pans 2" to 3" deep and bake in oven 180⁰ for 2 hours. Let cool and bag in plastic bags and close tightly. This sterilized soil will have no weed seeds, no fungus diseases and will keep damp and ready to use for several months. It gives off an unpleasant odour while in the oven so many members like to do enough to get them through a season all at the same time. Most members use this mixture for starting seeds under lights.

Mixture for Starting Seeds Without Soil:
When sowing seed you may use a half and half mixture of peat moss and perlite. No soil is required at this stage. Soil which has not been sterilized will only increase the risk of "damping off" which is a fungus disease attacking the base of the stem of the tiny seedlings. Get your peat moss and perlite damp before sowing the seed. This is most easily accomplished with hot water. A one inch depth of sowing medium is sufficient at this stage. Get it as level as you can and for really small seeds sift a top layer onto your seed flat through a piece of window screening.

Sow the seed just as thin as you can in straight lines about 1" apart. The bigger seeds can be covered with a thin layer of your mixture, just sufficient to hide the seed, but the smaller seed should not be covered at all. Most of the smaller seed needs light to germinate and if it is covered it will severely delay and reduce germination.

When the seed is sown and labelled it should be watered by setting the seed flat in a trough of lukewarm water until you can just see a faint beading of moisture on the surface, when it should be removed promptly before it is too soggy wet. If you wish you may add a fungicide to the water at this stage as a one-time treatment to prevent damping off disease.

When the seed flat has drained it should be covered with a sheet of glass or transparent plastic and placed in a warm location for germinating. It is most important not to let the seed flats dry out during germination but, if the cover is left in place it should not require watering again until germination has occurred. As soon as the seeds are up the plastic must be removed promptly and the flat moved to a light bright cooler location. Watch them closely and when they are dry on top they must be watered from below again with lukewarm water, but remember to remove the flat from the water trough before it is saturated. No further fungicide should be needed and no fertilizer at this stage. Try to keep them on the dry side and as cool as possible.

When they have 2 pairs of leaves or are big enough to handle, whichever comes first, seedlings should be transplanted to another container where they have plenty of room to develop. Any container at least 2½" deep may be used provided it has good drainage. At this stage one third soil may be added to your peat moss/perlite mixture if that's what you are using, and you may begin fertilizing with plant starter 10-52-10. This will encourage root development. Don't use a heavy nitrogen feed which will produce lots of greenery on top which you don't need at this stage. If your seedlings get too tall you may pinch out the top to develop side shoots, but if you have been able to maintain a temperature of 50-60°F they will stay stocky of their own accord. Remember that you can control growth by cultural conditions more than by chemicals. If you can run them cool, hungry and dry you can produce a better plant. If growth is too slow and you want to speed them up, apply heat, water and fertilizer and you will get startling results.

Seeds of different annuals are very different in their individual requirements, some insisting on darkness to germinate and others benefiting greatly by supplemental light giving them sixteen hours of light. Germination times and light and temperature requirements for a few of the most common annuals are listed at the end of this chapter.

Planting outside must be preceeded by a period of acclimatization or "hardening off". Set plants out in the shade all day when temperature is over 40°F and put them somewhere COOL at night. DON'T bring them back into the house where they will be "nice and warm" or put them in the basement until you can plant them out. All they need is protection from actual freezing such as an unheated garage. Water only sufficiently to prevent wilting during this period. Withholding water helps to toughen the tissues and produce a dark green stocky plant which will be able to withstand stress conditions. The east side of the house or a shed is best where they will be protected from wind and late afternoon heat. A cold frame is the ideal situation where they can have the lid closed on them at night and opened all day, rain or shine. Don't baby them too much.

When the time comes to plant out, do so in the evening or on a cool day. Water immediately. You may add fertilizer to the water such as a tablespoon of 10-52-10 per gallon of water. Once you have placed your seedling in the garden firm up the soil around it, and if the weather clears or the wind comes up, cover it with an overturned flower pot to protect it, for hot sun or strong winds can devastate young transplants. Anytime you notice your seedlings are wilting, cover them for a few hours until they are strong enough to withstand the weather. In more unprotected gardens encircle your transplant with a milk carton or tin can from which both ends have been removed, and leave on until the plant outgrows it.

Some annuals can be sown directly outdoors in the spring. These are noted in the list of recommended types of annual flowers further on in this chapter. For those who do not have the space or the time to start seeds indoors, and who do not wish to go to the expense of purchasing bedding out plants, these annuals will be of great service to them.

Location of your flower beds is an important consideration for all flowers have different needs. Some like full sun, others prefer a moist area. Nearly all need some shelter so awareness of the prevailing winds in your area is important. If you have flower beds on each side of your house, consider the following factors. The south and west walls of your house receive the most sun, while the east wall receives the early morning sun and is warmed up first. The north wall receives very little. Thus your north bed is good for shade-loving plants; your east bed for plants requiring a long day, semi-shade and good protection from the wind; your south bed for annuals loving hot, dry conditions; and, your west bed for flowers which will tolerate afternoon heat. Your house will also offer some protection against frost as houses lose heat through their walls which flows out over the adjacent flower beds.

When trying to determine where to locate flower beds in your garden which will be away from your house, consider the amount of shelter they will receive, the degree of shade, and the drainage which would be provided by each location. We suffer from late spring and early fall frosts in our area so it is a good idea not to put beds in low-lying areas as that is where frost will settle.

At the end of the growing season remove dead annuals from your beds as they may contain insect eggs, add fresh loam, well-rotted manure, and peat moss and sand if your soil is too heavy. Dig the garden roughly to allow for greater moisture absorption. Large clumps of soil should be left as winter's frost will break them down. In the spring when the soil is dry enough remove any debris and dig the beds well to thoroughly mix in your fall coverings of manure, etc. Smooth the beds with a rake to help maintain the moisture level.

The following is a list of recommended annual flowers grown successfully in our area. (Those marked with '*' are self seeding so will come up year after year if conditions are favourable.)

Type	When to Plant	Location
African Daisy	indoors, early May	dry area, full sun
Ageratum	indoors, early April	full sun
Alyssum	indoors, early April	full sun
Aster	indoors, late March	full sun
Baby Blue Eyes (Nemophilia)	seed directly in garden	full sun
*Bachelor Button	seed directly in garden	grows anywhere
Bartonia	seed directly in garden	full sun
Bells of Ireland	indoors, early April	full sun
*Calendula	seed directly in garden	full sun

Type	When to Plant	Location
California Bluebell (Phacelia)	seed directly in garden	full sun
*California Poppy	seed directly in garden	poor soil, full sun
Calliopsis	indoors, early April	full sun
Candytuft	seed directly in garden	grows anywhere
Clarkia	seed directly in garden	full sun or semi-shade
Convolvulus Tricolor	indoors, mid March	full sun or semi-shade
*Cosmos	seed directly in garden	warm spot
Dianthus	indoors, early April	dry area, poor soil
Dusty Miller	indoors, mid March	grows anywhere
Gazania	indoors, mid March	full sun
Gloriosa Daisy	indoors, early March	full sun
Godetia	seed directly in garden	sunny position
Larkspur (Annual)	seed directly in garden	full sun or semi-shade
Linaria	seed directly in garden	grows anywhere
Livingstone Daisy (Mesembryanthemum)	indoors, early April	full sun, poor soil
Lobelia	indoors, early March	cool location
Marigold	indoors, see chart p. 80	full sun
Mimulus	indoors, early April	full sun or semi-shade
Mignonette	seed directly in garden	full sun or semi-shade
Nasturtium	seed directly in garden	full sun or semi-shade
Nemesia	indoors, early April	semi-shade or full sun
Nicotiana	indoors, early March	semi-shade
Ornamental Kale	indoors, mid April	grows anywhere
Pansy	indoors, early March	grows anywhere
Petunia	indoors, early March	full sun or semi-shade
Phlox	indoors, early April	semi-shade
Pincushion Flower (Scabiosa)	indoors, early April	full sun or semi-shade
Portulaca	indoors, mid March	full sun, warm spot
Queen Anne's Lace	seed directly in garden	full sun
Rudbeckia	indoors, early April	full sun
Salpiglossis	indoors, early April	full sun or semi-shade
Schizanthus	indoors, early April	full sun or semi-shade
*Shirley Poppy	seed directly in garden	dry area
Snapdragon	indoors, late March	full sun
Stocks	indoors, early April	full sun
Strawflower	indoors, early April	sunny position
Sweet Pea	sow early in garden	full sun or semi-shade
*Tidy Tips	seed directly in garden	full sun
Verbena	indoors, mid March	full sun
Viscaria	indoors, mid March	full sun

It is too cold in this area to grow plants commonly recommended for shade such as coleus and impatiens which is why they are not on the above list. We recommend nicotiana, pansies and other annuals on the list which state semi-shade.

A Member's Planting Dates for Annual Seeds

Planting dates for starting annual seeds indoors for home consumption which I have found to be satisfactory are as follows. Note: anyone growing plants for sale would have to start their seeds earlier in order for their plants to be large and attractive enough to sell. For your own use, smaller plants will set out and grow better than bigger plants.

Flowers:

March 10 to 15	Pansy, single petunia, snaps, wallflower, lobelia
March 18 to 25	Asters, statice, larkspur, dianthus, salpiglossis
April 1 to 5	Nicotiana, mimulus, scabiosa, calliopsis, cosmos, rudbeckia rustic, quaking grass, phlox, nemesia
April 10 to 15	Stocks, strawflowers, gilia, lavatera, large marigolds, paprika marigold
April 20	Calendula
May 1	Dwarf marigold, african daisy

Vegetables:

March 10	Celery, leeks, Spanish onions
April 1	Lettuce, early tomatoes
April 15	Cauliflower, brussels sprouts, broccoli

Sweet Peas
Tom Davenport's Method

Plant seed around April 10-15. Before planting soak seeds for 24 hours by which time most of them will be swollen and ready to break open, any that are not are nicked on the side opposite the lifeline.

Plant in 3" peat pots containing a mixture of potting soil, peat moss and vermiculite. Put 3 or 4 seeds in each pot a half an inch deep and cover with soil. Water well, cover with black plastic and put in a warm place until the seeds germinate and you can see green tips peeking through the soil (10 days to 2 weeks). Remove immediately to a cooler spot (around 50°F). You may wish to separate the plants in the peat pots into individual pots before transplanting outdoors. When 4 leaves have formed, plant tips should be pinched off after selecting one strong shoot which will remain as a leader; or, if you only have a few plants of one colour let 2 shoots grow. Plants may be hardened off in a cold frame.

Select a fairly sunny spot with a good depth of topsoil for planting your sweet peas. Dig a trench from 12" to 18" deep and add well-rotted manure and bone meal to the bottom of the trench, mixing it well with the soil as you fill it in. Add bone meal alone to the top 8" mixing it in well also. Let it settle before transplanting your plants.

Sweet peas need a support fence on which to climb. Chicken wire stretched between posts set in at each end of the row works very well. Rows should run north to south and on either side of each support fence so 2 rows can be supported by 1 fence. Between the double rows you should leave 3' of space to the next double row.

Sweet peas should be planted 2" deeper than required. Fill in the trench as they grow. Transplanted plants should be planted at ground level. Plants should be 8" apart in the row.

In order to grow beautiful, long-stemmed sweet peas the tendrils are removed carefully and the stems are tied to the support fence with tie-ons or attached with fine metal rings which you can purchase. This must be done each morning. Removing the tendrils allows more strength to go into the bloom and also makes for straighter stems.

When the plants are approximately 18" high, the ties are loosened carefully from the supports and plants. The vines are then laid on the ground for about half their length. The other half is gently bent back up again and retied to the support fence. This process, which is called layering, gives the plants greater strength and is said to improve the quality of the bloom.

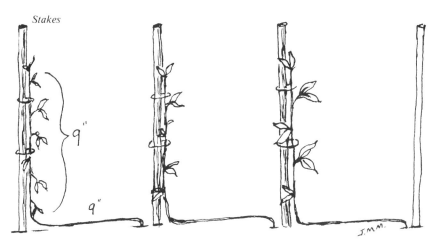

Layering Sweetpeas

Sweet peas like lots of water so don't spare the hose.

Biennials

Plants which take two seasons to complete their growing cycle are called biennials. They die after blooming and producing seed. However, as they self-seed they can continue to bloom year after year. All biennials stay green over the winter and should be protected as described under perennials. Biennials which are commonly grown in our area are as follows:

CANTERBURY BELL *(Campanula calycanthema)* - can be grown from seed - during the first summer will grow as green plants - will bloom second year and reseed themselves. Colours range from blue and pink to white. Height 2 ft.

FORGET-ME-NOT *(Myosotis)* - blue blooms in early June at the same time as tulips. Height 8 ins.

HOLLYHOCK *(Alathea rosea)* - plant in sunny sheltered spot - doesn't like wind - summer blooming - needs staking - old fashioned single kind is hardiest, the hybrid doubles not always surviving the winter without adequate protection. Colours: red, white, pink and yellow. Height 6 ft. A shorter annnual kind can be started in March indoors and will bloom the first year.

SWEET ROCKET *(Hesperis matronalis)* - grows all over Christendom - purple strongly-perfumed flowers. Height 30 ins.

SWEET WILLIAM *(Dianthus barbatus)* - likes a sunny spot - loves lime - blooms early summer - must be covered for winter - sprinkle wood ashes around plants. Height 30 ins.

VIOLA - prolific - small variety called Johnny Jump Up - can become a nuisance - will grow anywhere.

Viability of Seeds

It is not a good idea to keep your left-over seeds more than one year. Usually you can use them up the second spring in any case. Germination percentage and vigour of seedlings decreases with each year and depends greatly on type of seed and storage conditions.

Seed should be stored in a cool, dark, dry place in a cardboard box. If stored in airtight tins or polythene bags they will form condensation and rot. Dampness is fatal. Mark the year of purchase on each stored packet.

Old seed should be given a germination test 3 weeks before sowing the main batch. Fill a jar half full of damp soil, and put 10 seeds on a piece of damp paper towel on top of the soil. Put the lid on tightly, set in good light and see how many germinate. It is not necessary to grow them any further than the germination stage. This saves discovering too late that they will not germinate and missing three weeks of our short growing season while you wait to be certain they are not coming up.

It is hard to generalize because each kind of seed has different require-ments. Some need to be fresh from the plant for successful germination. Others need 6 months of rest or a freezing period to break dormancy. Some stay viable for many years, and indeed seeds found deep within a glacier having been deep frozen for hundreds of years have germinated upon being sown.

The following list names some seeds which I have found to lose vigour very quickly and which should be used their first year.

Flowers:

Alyssum	Hollyhock	Nicotiana
Canterbury Bell	Kochia	Portulaca
Delphinium	Nemesia	Salvia

Vegetables:

Chives
Lettuce
Onions

These seeds I have found to last for more than 2 years. Seedling vigour did not decrease noticeably and germination was extremely good up to 4 years.

Flowers:

African Daisy	Marigolds	Snapdragon
Cosmos	Pansy	Sweet Pea
Daisy	Petunia	

Vegetables:

Beans	Cabbage	Radish
Beets	Cauliflower	Spinach
Broccoli	Pea	Swiss Chard

Nearly all seeds will germinate at a fairly good percentage the second year provided that they have been stored under the proper conditions, but to keep them longer is asking for problems.

Germination Timetable for Popular Annuals

Variety	Light Requirements	Days to Germinate	Soil Temp. to Germinate	Temp. to Grow Seedlings	Weeks to Grow**
Ageratum	Light	5	70°F	60°F	10
Aster	*	8	70	60	6
Alyssum	*	5	70	50	10
Dusty Miller	Light	10	75	60	16
Dianthus	*	4	70	50	8
Dahlia	*	5	70	50	6
Lobelia	*	20	70	50	16
Marigold (Tall African)	*	5	70	50	6
Marigold (French dwf.)	*	5	70	50	8
Marigold (Large fl. dwf.)	*	5	70	50	10
Nemesia	Dark	5	65	50	12
Nicotiana	Light	20	70	60	8
Pansy	Dark	10	65	50	20
Petunia (Single)	Light	10	70	55	12
Petunia (Double)	Light	10	70	55	16
Portulaca	Dark	10	70	60	10
Snapdragons	Light	10	65	50	12
Verbena	Dark	20	65	50	10
Cabbage Family	*	5	70	50	6
Onions	Dark	5	75	50	20
Tomatoes	Dark	10	75	50	8

*Will germinate in either light or dark
**This means weeks from sowing of seed until plant is ready to set out in the garden. These figures are for greenhouse conditions. For windowsill gardeners, reduce the time by one third.

 **Helpful Hints**

Keep oil drums in the garden area and fill with water. By the time the water is applied to the garden it has been nicely warmed by the sun.

When you are transplanting tall leggy plants, lay the plants out at a 45° angle and cover all but the growing tip (top 4 leaves) with soil.

Notes

Chapter Eight

Perennials

Planning:

It is a great art to plan a perennial border well. The blooms are spectacular and colourful, but each has its own blooming period of 3-6 weeks, then it is finished for the season. Some bloom in early summer, and others don't start until late July or August. Another group does not begin flowering until September but these are usually too late blooming to be worthwhile planting in this area. You should draw a plan on paper to figure out heights, blooming times and colours as well as the mature size of the plants. Either blend the colours and varieties so that there is always something blooming, which can give a rather spotty appearance, or else have a spring display and a summer bed so that there is a great mass of colour with several types of plants all doing their thing at once in a certain area. Remember that only man makes straight lines. Nature prefers curves.

Texture of leaves also adds a lot of interest to the perennial bed. Sword-shaped leaves of the iris contrast well with more bushy greenery. A few grey-leaved plants such as artemesia or pinks add an interesting colour variation.

The most important requirement perennials have is good drainage. Usually they do not require any particular type of soil and most do well in full sun or semi-shade.

On Facing Page
Top left: Pacific Giant delphinium, in foreground heliopsis.
Top right: Dahlias.
Centre left: Bearded iris.
Centre right: Clematis.
Bottom left: Early spring tulips.
Bottom right: Lilies.

Propagation:

Perennials can be started from stem and root cuttings, division of the parent plant, or from seed. If you plan to start seed indoors bear in mind that most perennial seed will germinate better if prefrozen for 48 hours, unless otherwise stated on the packet. After removing the seed packet from your freezer sow the seed immediately. This freezing process is known as stratification. Perennials which are not easily raised from seed and are better propagated by division or layering are: peonies, bleeding heart, daylilies, iris, trollius and clematis. Generally, it is best to sow perennial seed outdoors in a nursery bed in the spring when the soil has warmed up. The following spring the plants can then be moved to their permanent position where they will come into bloom.

Take note of the blooming time of each type of perennial before making plant divisions. It is a general rule that perennials which bloom in the spring, such as bleeding heart or Oriental poppies, should be transplanted in early fall to give them enough time to develop established roots before the ground freezes. Summer-blooming plants should be divided in the spring before too much growth has occurred on the parent plant (new growth should be less than 6" high).

When dividing perennials preserve as much root as possible from the outer perimeter of the clump and discard the old center portion. Do not allow those with fibrous roots to dry out. Tubers and rhizomes should be divided with a very sharp knife and the cut should be allowed to callous over before planting.

When you receive plant divisions check for disease, pests, and weeds which must be removed before planting. Some gardeners recommend soaking the roots in a bucket of lukewarm water before planting as the best means of cleaning the plants of weeds and grass.

Culture:

In the spring you should dig around your perennials and remove any quack grass or other perennial weeds, for if they get established it is almost impossible to get rid of them. The most efficient way to remove quack grass is by painting a systemic grass killer on the grass using extreme care not to drop any on the surrounding plant as shown on next page.

Wind and rain can do a great deal of damage to your taller perennials so it is wise to stake them. The best time to do this is before too much growth has taken place on your plants. The leaves will then grow and conceal the stakes and ties. Make sure your stakes are long enough to allow for future growth. Perennials such as peonies may be supported by the use of wire cages.

When watering your perennials give them a thorough soaking to encourage deep root growth.

When applying systemic herbicides wear rubber gloves and use a milk carton cut lengthwise to catch drips.

Winter Care:

Not all the perennials grown in our area are fully hardy, thus without winter protection they will not survive. In the fall, after hard frost has stopped all growth, cut back your perennials, leaving about a 10 inch stubble to catch the snow and hold your protective mulch, which may be leaves, well-rotted manure, straw or branches.

Leaves make a good mulch. They are available at the right time of year and provide good insulation, but will all blow away unless you cover them with loose branches or old chicken wire. A layer of rotted barnyard manure over your beds gives winter protection and provides nutrients in the spring. (Note: Peonies, delphiniums, lilies and iris do not like manure.) Barnyard manure also improves the texture of the soil. Straw has its drawbacks as one of our members points out: "It attracts mice which burrow in it which inevitably results in the destruction of my best plants." If you share these problems perhaps it would be best to cover your evergreen perennials with just a layer of loose branches.

Many types of perennials are grown successfully in our area. They are listed as follows, with comments from our members. We hope they will be of use to you:

ACHILLEA: (a) *A. ptarmica* (Bridal Wreath) - clusters of white pom-pom flowers on 2' high plants. Spreads rapidly.

(b) *A. millefolium roseum* (Pink Yarrow) - ferny leaves - deep pink flowers in August and September, unharmed by frost - make good dried flowers.

(c) *A. filipendula* (Gold Plate) - flat-topped yellow flower clusters, dries well - tends to spread.

BABY'S BREATH *(Gypsophila paniculata)*: blooms in summer - needs space - doesn't like shade - very useful in flower arrangements.

BALLOON FLOWER *(Platycodon):* blue and white, blooms early August - good for cutting but singe stem. Before opening, flower looks like a balloon.

BEGONIAS: are covered in a special section at the end of this chapter

BERGENIA: evergreen leaves provide good fall colouring. One of the earliest flowering - pink hyacinth-like blooms. Likes a humusy soil. Leaves 10" high, flowers 18" high. Tolerates shade.

BLEEDING HEART:

> (a) *Dicentra spectabilis:* blooms vigourously in any exposure and blooms early thus should be transplanted in late August. Requires soil rich in humus - does not like peat moss. Useful for shady places. Pink flowers - height 3 feet.
>
> (b) Fernleaf *(D. eximia)*: blooms all summer. Dainty ferny leaves, rose-pink blooms. Height 12". Tolerates shade.

BUTTERCUP (Double) *(Ranunculus acris florapleno)*: yellow flowers throughout the summer. Soil should contain some sand - will grow and bloom in a shady area. Height 2'.

CHINESE LANTERN *(Physalis franchettii)*: seed pods turn a striking orange colour in the fall and are lovely in dried arrangements. Spreads rapidly. Height 2'.

CAMPANULA: (a) *C. carpatica* (Carpathian Bell Flower) - neat mound of heart-shaped leaves with blue or white bells in July and August - height 8".

> (b) *C. glomerata* (Clustered Bell Flower) - vivid purple cluster of flowers on top of 12" stem - good to plant in a spot where you don't want to grow anything else as it will spread.
>
> (c) *C. persicifolia* (Peach Leaf Bell Flower) 3 feet tall clumps of blue or white bell flowers.
>
> (d) *C. pyramidalis* (Chimney Bell Flower): 4' tall narrow spires of blue or white flowers.

CLEMATIS: are covered in a special section at the end of this chapter.

COLUMBINE *(Aquilegia):* blooms in early summer in a wide range of colours - can prolong bloom if seed pods are picked off - does not like peat moss. Transplant when small - best started from seed. Slugs will devour the young plants in a wet year. Happy in sun or shade.

CONE-FLOWER *(Rudbeckia laciniata)*: variety called Golden Glow bears a lovely yellow flower on a very tall plant - needs staking. Blooms in August - spreads rapidly.

CORAL BELLS *(Heuchera sanguinea)*: bears a dainty red flower on 12" stems above a rosette of evergreen leaves - needs winter protection. Blooms all summer. Does well in a rockery.

COREOPSIS: golden yellow daisy type flower, good for cutting. Keep soil moist and seed pods picked to extend blooming time into late summer. Height 2'.

DAHLIAS: are covered in a special section at the end of the chapter.

DAYLILIES *(Hemerocallis)*: easily grown. Require lots of space, moist soil, good drainage. Bloom profusely if they find conditions they like. Older peach and yellow varieties spread rapidly - modern varieties of different colours stay within bounds. Height 2'.

DELPHINIUMS: plant in a protected area away from winds - do not mulch or use manure. Pacific Giant variety recommended - a 4' high variety called Blue Fountains is better for a more exposed place, though these too need staking. Watch for caterpillars in the centre of the developing buds in early spring. Wood ashes sprinkled around the plants will help repel bugs.

DIANTHUS: do well in rockeries. All need a well-drained location and will not tolerate sitting in a puddle when the snow melts. Carry their leaves above ground all winter and are attractive to deer and rodents. Most common kinds are:

   (a) *D. Arenarius* (Sand pink) - a tight cushion mound, covered in starry white flowers in June.
   (b) *D. caesius* (Cheddar pink) - cushion mound of grey leaves, pink single flowers in June and July.
   (c) *D. chinensis* (Baby doll) - 6" high, blooms first year, mixed colours.
   (d) *D. deltoides* (Maiden pink) - a creeping mat of dark green leaves with deep red single flowers in July.
   (e) *D. plumaris* (Clove pink) - looks like a small carnation - good perfume - blooms in June.

EDELWEISS *(Leontopodium):* good rockery plant - strange furry white star-shaped blooms in July and August - very hardy.

GREAT LEAF GOLDEN RAY *(Ligularia)*: grows in the shade - needs staking - very tall - yellowish/orange flowers - very hardy.

HARDY GLOXINIA *(Incarvillia)*: very lovely - rose pink blooms. Plant in semi-shade where soil remains moist. Also known as Garden Gloxinia.

HELIOPSIS: double yellow flower in July and August Likes full sun. Height 3'.

ICELAND POPPY *(Papaver nudicaule)*: the Lake Louise poppy - blooms from spring to fall - easily grown from seed planted directly in the garden in May. Lovely shades of yellow and orange - frost resistant - hates to be moved.

IRIS: (a) Bearded: thrives in full sunlight and should be in a well-drained area - transplant in August by laying rhizomes on soil surface and burying roots. Should be divided every 3-5 years. Use bonemeal, not manure, for fertilizer. The beardless varieties of iris are moisture-loving.

(b) Siberian Iris (grassy-leaved iris): also love moisture and do well around pools and ponds, or in soil with a high humus content. Keep these broken up or they will become root bound and will not bloom.

(c) *Reticulata and Danfordiae* are dwarf iris which grow from bulbs and reach 4-6 inches in height. Plant bulbs in fall - they are perfectly hardy - will bloom in spring.

JACOB'S LADDER *(Polemonium caeruleum)*: completely hardy - blooms in early summer - blue or white flowers - 2 feet high. Is happy in full sun or semi-shade.

LILIES: are covered in a special section at the end of this chapter.

LILY OF THE VALLEY *(Convallaria)*: these lovely, fragrant bell-shaped flowers make a good ground cover in a problem shaded area. Spread rapidly.

LINUM: also known as wild blue flax. Delicate flowers in a beautiful pale shade of blue which open only in the morning. Seeds itself - hates to be moved. Height 18 inches.

LUPINE: does not like lime - prefers heavy soil. Transplant when very young - blooms in July.

LYTHRUM: these graceful plants with their pink flower spikes bloom in August - Morden Pink variety most commonly grown. Height 4-6 feet.

MALTESE CROSS *(Lychnis chalcedonica)*: blooms in July and August - clusters of star-shaped bright red flowers on 3 foot high plants. Should be staked. Likes full sun and lots of moisture - attracts hummingbirds.

MEADOW RUE *(Thalictrum aquilegifolium)*: a fluffy cloud of light purple blooms in early summer - sun or partial shade - likes rich, humusy soil. Height 3-4 feet.

MICHAELMAS DAISY *(Aster)*: hardy aster - blooms late summer. Are many different varieties.

MONKSHOOD *(Aconitum napellus)*: dark blue or blue and white - very hardy. Blooms in July and August - should be staked. Poisonous. Height 4 feet.

MOUNTAIN BLUET *(Centaurea montana)*: the perennial form of Batchelor's Button. Rather floppy but lovely colour blue early in the summer. Height 18 inches.

ORIENTAL POPPY *(Papaver orientalis)*: blooms in May and June - very large blooms - most common colour orange with black centre. Bees love them. 2-3 feet tall.

OX-EYE DAISY *(Chrysanthemum leucanthemum)*: a dependable self-seeding perennial, single and double, which provides a splash of white in the hottest part of summer. Perfectly hardy and drought resistant - seeds itself all over. Height 12 inches.

PAINTED DAISY *(Pyrethrum)*: needs to be staked. Prefers sunny open spot and well-drained soil. Shades of white, red and pink. Blooms in early summer then has leaves which are rather untidy and should be trimmed back. Height 2-3 feet.

PENSTEMON: also likes sunny well-drained locations. Tall spikes of foxglove-like flowers in July and August, pink and white shades. Subject to mildew in late summer. Height: up to 3 feet. Annual varieties are also available.

PEONY: long-lived perennial with a lovely fragrance. Needs good soil and must not be allowed to dry out - likes open sunny areas, but will tolerate a little shade so long as it is not competing with tree roots. Needs to be staked. Large fully double blooms in red, pink or white. Plant in late August, not more than 2'' deep - top dress with wood ashes or bonemeal - they do not like manure. Hate to be moved and will sulk for years when disturbed. Leave ants alone as some say they assist in blossom opening. Height: up to 3 feet.

PHLOX: (a) *P. paniculata* (perennial or English phlox): large heads of flowers on 3 foot tall stems - should be staked. White seems to be the hardiest colour. Likes a dressing of well-rotted manure and rich moist soil - must be covered in the fall for winter protection - needs lots of space and a little shade. Mulch to protect shallow roots and conserve moisture. Doesn't like wet leaves, especially at night time, so don't water overhead. Watch for spider mites and mildew.

(b) *P. subulata* (moss phlox): good in rockeries - creeping plant covered with flowers in May and June in shades of pink, white or red. For the rest of the season provides green ground cover of leaves which do not die back in winter. Must be in a well-drained location and have winter protection.

(c) *P. borealis* (Arctic phlox): very similar to subulata (above) but more succulent leaves with a neat shiny dark green appearance.

PRIMROSE *(Primula)*: dwarf varieties are fine for rockeries, shady places, or woodland gardens. Require a rich humusy damp soil - must have shade, except for *P. auricula* which can stand more sun than the others. Some varieties bloom in early spring, others in June and July. Hardiest types are: *Primula veris* (polyanthus); *P. auricula; P. cortusoides* (Fairy Primrose); *P. denticulata* (Globe Primrose) and *P. eliator* (Ox Lip).

SHASTA DAISY *(Chrysanthemum maximum)*: easily grown from seed. Tall, hardy plants providing large showy white daisies with yellow centres. Bloom mid-summer till fall - like heavy rich soil. Watch for aphids. Height 3 feet.

TROLLIUS: yellow or orange buttercup-like flowers. Bloom in early spring. Likes cool moist soil and some shade. Height 1-2 feet.

VERONICA: (a) *V. spicata* (Speedwell): narrow green leaves and blue flower spikes. Likes sunny well-drained soil - good for flower arrangements. Very hardy - bees and humming-birds love it. Height 2 feet.

(b) *V. incana:* grey woolly leaves, small blue flower spikes - good for rockeries. Height 12 inches.

(c) *V. repens:* creeping moss-like plant with brilliant blue flowers and glossy dark green leaves. Height 4 inches.

Tuberous Rooted Begonias
by Dessa Macklin

Tuberous begonias are among the most satisfactory plants. They provide beautiful blossom continuously through summer and fall.

There are two types, one having large blooms, both double and single, and the pendulous, a smaller hanging variety. The latter is most suitable for hanging baskets of any kind. Begonias have a wide range of beautiful colours ranging from pink to red, various shades of yellow, orange, and of course white. They also vary in form. Some resemble carnations, others roses, still others camellias which are large and exotic.

A good time to start these plants is in late March which can be done by planting individual tubers or you may put several in a large container. They start very well in peat moss in a warm place such as on top of the refrigerator where the temperature will not go over 80°F. When growth is four inches or so, each plant can be replanted into larger pots, baskets, or a well sheltered spot in the garden. They like a rich planting mixutre; one third well-rotted manure, one third good garden loam and the rest peat moss with leaf mould if possible. Plant tubers firmly and cover with about an inch of soil. They like an eastern exposure which provides morning sun. Protection from wind is essential, as they break very easily. They need fertilizer about every three weeks. All purpose plant food, 15-30-15 or fish fertilizer will do nicely. They take a lot of water in hot weather and will bloom continuously through until it is time to bring them in to escape frost. Allow tubers to dry out in soil in which they have been growing, which they will do after foliage dries off. Remove, shake off soil, and spread out to dry for a few days. Before storing, dust tubers with a good bulb dust. Put in separate plastic bags covered with dry peat moss, seal and store in cold room until the following spring. Remember to label as to color and variety.

Bulbs
by Anne Vale

As soon as your annuals are cut down by the first heavy frost you should be planting your fall bulbs. The earlier you can get them in, the better the flowers will be next spring. It is no good waiting until spring and then going to your garden centre when you see your neighbour's bulbs in bloom. The first bulbs come on the market some time in September and the sooner you get there the better choice of colour and type you will have. Budget-minded gardeners can pick up half price bargains late in October, but by that time you may have to chisel a hole in the ground with an ice pick to plant them.

Bulbs like rich soil which is well drained. They will not tolerate sitting in a puddle in the spring. They will grow in sun or shade but those planted in full shade will bloom much later than the ones basking in full sun. If they are planted up against a basement wall, they will be awakened too early by the hot days in early spring and the flowers will be frozen. A little bit away from the wall is advisable, or out in the open away from the house. They will also be in less danger of drying out than if they are right against a south wall.

Of the bigger bulbs, tulips are most satisfactory. Daffodils are nearly always a disappointment. It is possible to grow them, but they bloom at the same time as the dandelions and their full yellow glory is lost. Hyacinths have been coaxed into bloom by some green thumb gardeners but are only borderline hardy. Tulips are easier and a sure-fire success even for beginning gardeners. If you choose your varieties carefully they will show colour over a period of 6 to 8 weeks in spring.

The first to bloom are the Kauffmania tulips. They are quite short with striped leaves and will bloom almost as soon as the snow melts. They are followed by the Fosteriana hybrids which include the familiar Red Emperor, a large-flowered brilliant scarlet, which does better out of the wind, as it is rather tall. A better choice for a windy place is the sweet little Red Riding Hood, or the peacock tulips, both only 6 to 8 inches high. They bloom very early, the same time as the scillas.

Species Tulips, the wild tulips from different parts of the world are also very early and make a lovely miniature rockery plant of great charm. Many have 4 or 5 flowers on one stem. The better bulb catalogues list quite a few hardy varieties well worth a try. Tulipa Tarda multiply rapidly and are completely hardy. They are only 4'' tall and covered in small yellow star-like blooms.

Following these in bloom are the single earlies, double earlies, and Triumph tulips. About 10 days later again the Darwin hybrids bloom, and then the Darwin tulips and cottage tulips round out the season. Another later flowering tulip is the lily flowering tulip with elongated pointed petals.

Plant your tulips at least 8'' deep. This way they will not come up too soon in the spring and will have a much longer life, only needing to be dug and divided about the fifth or sixth year. Otherwise they can be left in the ground and will reappear each spring without much help from you. At planting time you may give them a little bone meal which they enjoy but they don't need fertilizer at this stage and manure will only make them rot. The time for using a high phosphate fertilizer is after they have bloomed so that you build up the bulb for the following year. The leaves should not be removed until they have yellowed naturally.

When you have planted them, water the bed very thoroughly right till freeze-up and cover with a protective mulch so that it does not freeze too soon. Leaves raked from the lawn do very well as a mulch for bulbs. Twigs or chicken wire on top will stop it blowing away and it can be raked off again just before the leaves of the bulbs begin to poke up in spring.

Alliums are beginning to become available. These are flowering onions of various kinds and most are completely hardy. There is a yellow one, 12'' tall blooming in June *(Allium molyluteum)* and a very attractive white allium *(A. neopolitanum)* also 12'', June blooming. A strikingly different one is allium azureum, 2' tall with blue balls on top. *Allium ostrokianum* is a pink one, 12'' tall, blooming in July and is very hardy. They don't smell like onions unless you pinch them.

Three early blooming blue beauties are *Scilla siberica* (Siberian Squills), *Chionodoxa* (Glory of the Snow) and *Muscari* (Grape Hyacinths). They bloom one after the other in very early spring and if you mix all three of them together in a paper bag and then plant a patch somewhere you will have a sky blue carpet for at least 6 weeks in early spring. They are all about the same height and colour and multiply fast. *Scillas* and *Chionodoxa* will naturalize happily in a lawn and bloom before you cut the grass.

Snowdrops are not too successful. They want to bloom so early that they are tempted to come up in a chinook in January with the inevitable result. Aconites *(Eranthis hyemalis)* suffer the same way.

There are some dwarf Iris which are grown from a true bulb, not a rhizome. These are completely hardy and will pop up through the snow and bloom in late April. *Iris reticulata* (violet) and *Iris danfordiae* (yellow) are both only 4'' high.

Lilies are given their own section in this book and I need not describe them here except to say there are many hardy varieties which are grown in the foothills with great success.

Dutch crocus do well against some shelter. Mine are planted in front of a big rock which reflects the heat to them and they just love it. Stay away from the yellow ones. There again they bloom at the same time as the dandelions and don't show up as they should. In other climates they come much earlier and miss the competition provided by May dandelions.

I have tried English Bluebells *(Scilla campanulata)* several times but never had any success with them. I think it probably is too dry and cold for them. Anemones are not hardy over winter and must be started early in spring, the same as gladioli bulbs.

As a general rule of thumb plant all types of bulbs at a depth of 4 times the diameter of the bulb.

Clematis
by Theresa Patterson

This family of climbing vines are sensationally beautiful once they become established. They bloom over a long period from June to September producing hundreds of blossoms. Although they prefer to be planted on the east side of the house they will thrive in almost any exposure except west.

Clematis need cool roots so either grow small plants around the base to provide shade or cover the area around their feet with flat stones. They seem to like the lime from basement walls so do not dress with peat moss. Use compost or leaves instead. Fish fertilizer applied monthly really makes vigorous plants with quantities of blooms.

The vines need a sturdy trellis to climb on. Be sure to make it 10 or 12 feet high. Green plastic-covered chain link fence makes a dandy support for them.

In the late fall after the leaves are killed by frost, cut the vines down as they will shoot from the roots again in the spring. Be sure to keep them well watered all summer right up till freeze-up. After the ground is frozen cover them well with light branchy material such as the annuals you have pulled out of the bed in front of them.

The hardiest large-flowered variety for this area is Jackmanii, a lovely deep purple. Others which are extra hardy in this class are: Ville de Lyon (red), Ernest Markham - wine red, Comtesse de Bouchard (mauve), Ramona (blue), Lady Betty Balfour (blue and white), Huldine (white with a mauve stripe).

Smaller flowered species clematis are also successful and are followed by a cloud of feathery seed pods which are attractive through the fall. They are *Clematis tangutica,* a yellow bell-shaped flower, which grows wild in dry stony places and which is the only clematis which grows easily from seed. *Clematis ligustifolia* (white small flowers in early summer), and *Clematis verticellaris,* our native wild blue clematis which grows in shady areas and blooms in early June.

Dahlias
by Betty Nelson

Start dahlia tubers about the middle of April in a soil mixture of two parts soil, one part vermiculite and one part peat moss in containers with good drainage. Before planting divide up roots being sure to leave a growth eye on each piece. Plant in milk carton which is lying horizontally with one side cut out for the top and drain holes punched in the bottom. Plant so growth eye on tuber is at one end. If the tuber starts to sprout in mid winter this will exhaust the parent tuber but a cutting may be taken from the tip of this new growth, from which you may start a new plant. Tip cuttings may also be taken from any small growth sprouts which have appeared when you come to divide the tubers before planting. This way you get twice as many plants.

Plant in the garden about May 24th. Dig a hole larger and deeper than the milk carton, remove plant by cutting the side out of the carton, and slide plant and soil into the hole trying not to disturb the roots.

Place a support stake just behind the plant before filling in the hole and leave a depression around the plant to hold moisture. Cover on cold nights as plants will be about 8" high by this time and are susceptible to frost. Fertilize with 10-52-10 every three weeks or so at half strength. In dry weather deep water once a week. Gradually fill in the depression around the plants and tie to stakes as they grow up, for a wind can easily break their stems. Dahlias do best in a well-drained, fertile soil in full sunlight. They must also be in a sheltered spot. Cut off dead flowers and watch for pests as they are bothered by aphids, mites and some bug that nips the buds out when they just start to form.

When the tops have died down after frost, cut off the tops leaving about 2" top growth. Take up the tubers by digging well back from the plant because tubers will have grown sometimes a foot long under the soil surface, mostly horizontally.

Remove as much soil as possible. Turn upside down to drain hollow top and dry. When dry take ordinary household scissors and cut off all small roots. Place in dry peat moss or vermiculite in labelled plastic bags and store in cold room.

Fuchsia
by Anne Vale

These beautiful plants are surprisingly easy to grow. The secret is to give them as near Vancouver conditions as possible. They like to be outdoors and do not make a good houseplant. Indoors they will get long and straggly in growth and their flower buds will drop off. Find a location in part shade, such as under a tree or on the east side of the house, out of the wind. If you have such a location success is assured.

Start hardening them off in early spring by bringing them into a cool place which is protected from frost at night and setting them outside in the daytime. Gradually they will become used to cold nights with this treatment and be able to withstand several degrees of frost without harm. They like to be rained on, and should be hosed down regularly if no rain appears.

Soil mixture should be two parts soil, one part sand, two parts peat moss and should be kept on the damp side and fertilized at weekly intervals all summer with 20-20-20 fertilizer at a dilution of ½ tablespoon to a gallon of water.

In the autumn they should be brought in after the blooms and new growth have been exposed to a killing frost, and pruned hard back to the old wood; let them dry out and keep them cool and dark, watering only sufficiently to avoid dehydration to the point of no return. A root cellar or cold room is an ideal place for wintering fuchsia. If you have a greenhouse bring them out in March or earlier, put them in light, feed and water them so they will start into growth again. Pinch back the new growth when it is about six inches long and grow as cool and dry as possible until it is time to start hardening them off outdoors once more. If no greenhouse is available, put them in the house in your coolest lightest place. Fuchsias are very subject to pests. Hosing regularly will help but if whitefly or aphids are noticed put a pest strip among the branches and cover with a light weight plastic bag and put in a shady place for a day or two.

Fuchsias root easily from cuttings taken in early spring. When pinching back the new growth save the top two or three inches, remove the bottom pair of leaves, trim off neatly at a node, dip in rooting hormone and stick the cutting in a mixture of peat moss, vermiculite and sand, pull a plastic bag over its head and put in a warm place until rooted. This should take about three weeks.

Single varieties of fuchsia seem to bloom more prolifically than the doubles. There are many superb colour variations on the market.

Geraniums
by Norma Lyall

Propagation by Cuttings:

You will need: soil, vermiculite, peat moss, labels, a sharp knife or razor blade, rooting powder, pen, pencil and enough plastic bags to cover cuttings in pots.

Using 48 oz. juice cans measure two cans soil, 1 can coarse or medium vermiculite, and 1 can peat moss which has been soaked in hot rain or snow water, and mix them together. This mixture should be quite moist so it will hold its shape when you squeeze it, yet will still fall apart.

Using clean pots fill with moist soil mixture and clap the side of the pot to settle the soil. Put two cuttings in each two inch pot or four cuttings in each 4 inch pot. This way if one dies you still have plants in each pot.

Before you start taking cuttings separate all your colours and make sure you have enough labels for your pots so you know which colour is in each pot. Otherwise, if your geraniums are not in bud when it comes time to transplant them outdoors, you have no way of knowing what colour they are.

Cuttings may be made from February to September if they are in good sunlight. They should be taken from strong, healthy plants from which you have kept blooms and buds cut off so that all the strength has gone into the plant. Cut about ¼" to ½" below the node or leaf stem and remove all lower leaves and flower buds. A cutting only needs to be 2 to 4 inches long. Dip cuttings in rooting powder about ¼" deeper than they will be set in the soil, tapping off any excess powder. Taking the blunt end of the pencil, make a hole in the soil large enough to cover the node. Insert cutting and press soil around it to remove any air pockets. Cover the pot and cutting with a plastic bag and close with a twist tie. Place in a warm room with indirect light for 2 to 4 weeks.

Geranium Cutting

When cuttings have started to root or when you see leaves or shoots starting to appear, remove the bags and put the plants near sunlight. Check every day to make sure they are moist, for they must not be allowed to become dry. Geraniums don't like to be wet so don't overwater.

I have also had good luck starting cuttings in a tumbler of rain or snow water. In May of 1962 I received a 2 inch cutting from my aunt off a red and white geranium which I put in water. In 3 days it had a nice thick root on it, but this was unusual. Most times it takes 7 days or more in water. As soon as roots are about ½" long cuttings should be planted. Take great care not to break of these tender roots when planting. Use some potting mixture as for above and put the newly potted plants in plastic bags for 2 or 3 days. By the way, the red and white geranium had flowers on it by the end of June when I put it outside. I still have it - it has been a gem to me.

My mother grew lovely geraniums and she always used soil from pocket gopher mounds. Some say nothing will grow in this soil, but Mother always said gophers wouldn't dig in anything but good soil and her geraniums seemed to prove it.

Growing and Storage:

Before you put your tender new plants out in the garden you should harden them off by putting them in a cold frame or a porch where they won't freeze if we should have the odd frost at night. Geraniums seem to do very well on the east side of a building or fence. You may put them in the open if they are sheltered from winds. You should fertilize about every 2 weeks. Some people think fish fertilizer is the best and I do use it. I also use 20-20-20, 1 teaspoon per quart of water. Make sure you water first with clear water, or you can set your pot in a pan of fertilized water and leave it until you can see or feel moisutre on top of the soil. You then know the roots are moist and the fertilizer got to where it was needed. This method is fine if you only have a few plants. There are lots of good liquid plant foods, such as 10-15-10, which you may use with every watering if you make sure you follow the directions on the label. If you wish to keep your plants over winter do not fertilize after late August because the plants should be allowed to slow down and get ready for their dormant period.

If you have a greenhouse or a sunny room in which you may keep your plants blooming all winter, you can bring them in, fertilizing about once a month. If your plants are not already in pots or planters, dig them out of the garden and pot them. Keeping your favourite plants over winter saves money and most of the time they do better than new plants. If your plants do well the way you are treating them, keep up the good work. If not, try new ideas or methods to make your plants happy.

I put some plants in the basement in the dark, some I put in light and I have 4 or 5 pots in a south window which I use for cuttings. Some plants I put in our well which is like a root cellar. I leave them right in their pots. If the frost freezes these I still have some plants in the basement. I water the plants I keep in the basement when they are dry which is about every 2 weeks. I make sure not to get them too wet as the roots will rot. The plants in the well I don't water as it is very cool and damp.

Sometimes I cut plants back to about 6 or 8 inches when I bring them inside in the fall so they don't take up as much space. When little shoots start to appear in January or February, I put them in indirect light for a couple of weeks then I move them to direct sunlight later. If the sun is hot it will kill the tender sprouts. Don't forget to water at all times when needed but as I said don't get the plants too wet. A real good watering that gets to the roots is better than a little bit on top each day. A good practice is to water from the bottom once in a while by setting the pot in a pan of warm water. You may use half-strength fertilizer on these plants about every 3 weeks after they get 2'' or 3'' of growth. Test to see if plant has enough moisture by putting your finger in the soil about a ½''. If soil sticks to your finger or you can feel moisture then remove the pot from the pan.

If plants start to wilt they either need water, have too much water or it could be that they are getting too much heat. I like to shape my plants by pruning them early in spring with a good sharp knife or sharp pruning shears. Even though I have 2 pairs of these I use them so much that sometimes I can't find either of them. The cuttings you trim off your plants can be put back in the same pot. By trimming your plants they get a lot bushier and stand up to the wind much better than tall plants.

Good luck with your geraniums!

HELPFUL HINT:
In the fall dig up geraniums, shake dirt off roots, tie several plants together and hang upside down in the dark in your root cellar or cold room. In February put in individual pots and cut them back to about 5'' or 6''. Water and leave in the dark in the cold room for about a week. Gradually bring plants into the light. These plants may be put back in the garden in early June. If they are too woody, cut off the tops for cuttings and throw the old plant away.

Gladiolus
by Mary Poffenroth
Glads do best when planted in full sun. A light sand loam is ideal but they grow satisfactorily in almost any garden soil that has been enriched with compost, leaf mould or peat moss. A 5-10-5 fertilizer may be added. Avoid animal manures since they encourage bulb rot.

In this area bulbs should be planted in early May. For earlier blooming they may be soaked in water for about a week. Plant the bulbs about 4 to 6 inches apart, covering them with 4 to 6 inches of soil. A double row of bulbs is sometimes advantageous. I have found it successful to dig an 8'' wide trench, put leaf mould and bone meal (1 tablespoon/bulb) in the trench and make the double row by staggering the bulbs to achieve the proper spacing. Fertilize when the flower spikes appear and again after the flowers are picked.

When plants are about 12" tall hold them erect by "hilling up" the earth around the stems. Otherwise glads should be supported with stakes.

When picking the flowers leave 4 or 5 leaves on the plant so that the bulb can mature. To ensure stronger bulbs for another year permit only one flower to mature on each stock.

Dig up the bulbs, preferably about 4 weeks after frost. Cut off the tops and let the bulbs dry in an airy place out of the sun for 2 or 3 weeks. Remove the dried parts of the old bulb, dust with a combination insecticide-fungicide bulb dust and store in a cool place. Old nylon stockings make excellent storage bags since they can be hung up to allow air to circulate around them.

All different sized gladiolus flowers are available in early, medium and late flowering specimens. It is seldom worthwhile in this area to plant anything but the early flowering bulbs.

Lilies

by Betty Nelson

Most lily bulbs are planted in the fall just before the ground freezes. Plant where there is good drainage (if water puddles around them the bulbs will rot). Lilies like a good humusy soil, well prepared (no manure unless it is very well rotted). Plant bulb as soon as you get it - don't let it dry out. Plant small bulbs about twelve inches apart and cover with three or four inches of soil; large bulbs eighteen inches apart and covered with four to six inches of soil. Water as soon as planted. Fertilize plants with fertilizer high in nitrogen during the early growing season and later with fertilizer high in potassium for flower and bulb growth. Stake so the wind doesn't break them and don't let them get too dry. They like cool feet so mulch around plants or grow low annuals around them to shade the base of the lily plant. Remove dead lily flowers, don't let them go to seed. If cutting lilies for cut flowers, leave two thirds of the stem and leaves to feed the bulb (if you cut too much stem the bulb will die). I fall mulch with leaves, etc. to keep the ground from freezing and thawing.

Lilies take at least a month longer to produce bloom here so if the seller says they are June bloomers they will bloom in July; July in August. The so called August and September bloomers will be frozen while still in the bud stage. By planting varieties with specific blooming dates you can have lilies in bloom all summer. If they grow well in your location clumps will become crowded and will need to be divided up. They like a sunny location.

For further information on growing lilies I recommend the book *Let's Grow Lilies* by the North American Lily Society which may be obtained from: Canadian Prairie Lily Society, University of Saskatchewan, Saskatoon, Saskatchewan, S7N 0W0.

Wildflowers in the Garden

by Janet MacKay

Some wildflowers do very well under cultivation but so many of them become so rank they are almost like weeds.

I think the most successful flowers to transplant are the shooting stars. If you have a damp place they will grow up to twenty stems on a plant with sometimes as many as twenty blooms and buds on each. The stems are very thick and strong and the plants will last for years.

The blue violets are nice for about two years but then they have always died. I tried the white Canada violets one time but soon dug them out. They spread underground so fast they soon got out of hand. There is one little patch of yellow violets on our land. I tried transplanting a few but they just bloomed that year and never came up again.

The tall lungwort is another plant that gets too big under cultivation. They look so pretty in the woods with their pink buds and blue bells. In the garden the leaves are so big that they overwhelm the flowers. Also the harebells grow too many stems and flowers and they fall over.

I've tried to transplant the crocus but have never had them live. They have such a long tap root transplanting is next to impossible.

I have had very good luck with the two native junipers. The creeping juniper is very easy to start from a small piece. With the low juniper I think you need to get the whole plant. I've tried to transplant a small piece of it and didn't get it to grow.

The native ferns are very successful. We don't have the big ones in this country which grow further north. I have some on the north side of my house that are really very beautiful. The fronds are huge and so strong that they never fall over. A small fern does grow in this district where there are rocks. I have a few plants on the north side of the house and they have done very well.

Generally I think it is best not to transplant wild plants. They are difficult to transplant and do not do well under cultivation for the most part. Why not stay with domesticated plants for your gardens and appreciate wildflowers in their natural environment where they look so much more at home.

 **Helpful Hints**

Put wood ashes on delphiniums in early spring to prevent infestations of aphids.

Nylon stockings or J-Cloths make good ties for tall plants. Green yarn is good too and is inconspicuous.

To keep a supply of biennials such as Canterbury bells, hollyhocks, pansies etc. leave some blooms to go to seed. The following spring you will find seedlings around the old mother plant. Transplant as many as you need and hoe out the rest or they will take over your garden.

Cuttings from dahlias can be taken from tips of sprouts that form in late winter or early spring - a good way to increase your stock of plants.

Heat treatment helps to cure gladiola bulbs. Hang in nylon stockings over a heat register for 10 days.

Chapter Nine

Planters

Gardening Without a Garden
by Grace Bull

There are several reasons for gardening using pots, hanging baskets, planters and window boxes. Lack of space for a conventional garden, featureless house lines, short growing season, predators, old age or disabilities - all these can be overcome with container gardening. The main disadvantage is the fact that planters, etc. tend to dry out quickly and are usually so placed that they receive little or no rain so frequent watering is necessary.

Soil requirements are much the same for any container. A good potting mixture is half good rich soil, one quarter peat moss to retain mositure, one quarter perlite or vermiculite for porosity and a bit of bone meal or dried steer manure. All containers must have good drainage, but it's not necessary to always have holes in the bottom as there are places where dripping pots would not be desirable. Drainage can be achieved with a good layer of gravel or broken clay pots, covered with leaves or clean straw. It is better not to set containers on grass or bare ground since worms, etc. can invade the pots if there are drainage holes. A cement or gravel base is ideal. Large containers become very heavy when filled with soil - platforms of wood on casters can be used if you want to move planters from place to place. Some planters can be set on cement blocks for a tiered effect.

It is not necessary to change all the soil each year, especially in a fair

---

On Facing Page
Top left: Hanging basket containing fuchsia and trailing lobelia.
Top right: Red and pink petunias with alyssum in planter.
Centre: Hanging begonia.
Lower left: Pendulous begonia.
Lower right: Nasturtiums in cement block planter.

size container. However it is desirable to turn out the soil each spring, mix with some new rich soil, a bit of peat moss and a handful of steer manure and replace. In the case of hanging baskets however, because of their small size it is better to use fresh mixtures each year.

If a greenhouse or well lighted basement is available it is advantageous to plant up your planters early so that by the time the danger of frost is over you can put out an instant garden. In the fall the shelter and warmth of the house will give you blooms much longer than in the open. Smaller containers can be moved inside for protection from that first early frost. Perennials and small shrubs or trees are not successfully grown in pots in our climate. Remember that if you leave ceramic pots filled with soil outside in the winter, freezing and thawing are apt to break them.

Hanging Baskets: are used under eaves and under covered porches or patios. A windy location is not desirable. Hanging baskets can be of many types - sphagnum peat lined wire baskets are attractive but tend to dry out rapidly; plastic or wooden baskets are probably best. Be sure the hooks are solid and the wires or fine chains are secure. The best way to water hanging baskets is to place them in a tub of water until bubbles cease - if this is not convenient there are long handles with breaker nozzles which can be attached to your garden hose.

Some good plants for hanging baskets in full sun are ivy geraniums, african daisies, petunias (especially the cascade type), trailing lobelia and alyssum. Others that prefer shade are asparagus fern, nasturtiums, pendulous begonias, pansies and schizanthus (dwarf variety). In fact it is surprising how many garden flowers will trail if hanging which under normal growing conditions would not do so. In a well protected area many houseplants will benefit from a summer outside.

Tubs and Planters: Most any container can be used if it is of fair size; clay pots, and plastic pots are ideal but five gallon cans or tree containers from nurseries can be used. Roses, small dahlias, some of the more exotic but tender lilies, tiger flowers etc. can be grown in tubs. Lilies and dahlias can be lifted in the fall and stored over winter. Vegetables such as tomatoes, cucumbers, herbs and climbing beans can all be grown in containers. Many seed houses offer special patio types of vegetables. Any number of flowers can be used depending on your location - some of the better varieties for sun are geraniums of all types, african daisies, marigolds, petunias and in shady areas begonias and schizanthus. Don't forget to use alyssum, lobelia (both trailing and compact kinds) and dusty miller (dwarf variety such as silverdust) to fill in the pots around the edge and to trail over the sides.

Window Boxes: not only add interest to the outside of the house but have the advantage of being seen from within. Window boxes should be at least nine inches deep and about twelve inches wide, fastened securely and tipped slightly to the back. Cedar and fibreglass are excellent. The inside of wooden boxes may be treated with a wood preservative and the outside only can be painted. It is not necessary to have drainage holes if adequate drainage is provided, however if a metal liner is used it must have bottom holes. Use the same soil and drainage material as for other containers. Plants in individual pots can be set in the box and the area around filled with moss.

A nice combination for a window box in the sun is white marguerites, red or pink geraniums and trailing blue lobelia. Another is dwarf dusty miller, marigolds and white alyssum. On a shady side of the house begonias, coleus and asparagus fern are nice.

Remember the rules for successful container gardening are: rich soil, good drainage and adequate water as well as the proper choice of plants for their location.

Planters for Winter Beauty: some special tricks are discussed on pages 30 and 31.

 **Helpful Hints**

Put a layer of plastic in the bottom of hanging baskets to keep them from drying out so fast.

For any container use slow release fertilizer in planters and window boxes.

Chapter Ten

Rockeries

There is no getting away from it, rockeries are a lot of work. Why have a rockery? One reason is that it is a great way to tier a sloping garden or make good use of a natural contour. Another is to provide a setting for alpine plants which require a well-drained situation. Rockeries need not necessarily be on a bank but can equally well be laid out like an alpine meadow provided you have really well-drained soil which never collects puddles.

The rockery should be situated in the open, away from interfering tree roots. A shallow north-facing bank which gets oblique sun in summer but does not lose its snow in winter is ideal. East-facing is the next best location. If facing due south on a slope which is at right angles to the mid-day sun you will find that it bares off and dries out too quickly in winter and you will lose a lot of valuable plants.

The site should be prepared very carefully, since once your rocks and plants are in place it is very hard to get at the soil underneath to correct any problems. It does not get dug and manured at regular intervals like other flower beds and the soil must last the plants for the lifetime of the rockery. You should start by deeply digging the site. If quack grass is anywhere in the vicinity, you must clean it all out with the use of a systemic weed-killer of a type which will not contaminate the soil. You must also provide a physical barrier to prevent it creeping back in again. Well-rotted manure, bone meal and wood ashes should be liberally incorporated with the soil before placing the rocks.

The very first thing you have to do is make a plan on paper. Pace off

On Facing Page
Top left: Rockery of annual flowers.
Top right: Perennial rockery containing (top to bottom) Siberian iris, blue fescue, dianthus and variegated sedum.
Bottom: The bigger the area the bigger the rocks.

the area you are going to develop and try to draw it to scale on paper. Plan your plantings. Take a picnic up in the mountains and study how wild plants trail over rocks and fill crevices. With both types of rockeries remember to provide steps or pathways so that you have easy access to tend your plants.

Choose your rocks carefully. They should be large and porous with a flat surface. Field stones are not too good as they are round, slippery and non-porous. If you can find some sandstone with attractive lichen already growing on it so much the better. Remember that smaller porous rocks tend to be split by frost and will disintegrate.

Rockery on a Slope:

Set the rocks well into the soil with their flat surface uppermost, sloping them backwards so that any rain water falling on them will drain off back into the slope, instead of cascading off taking valuable topsoil along with it. Only about one-third of the rock should be visible. Pockets of soil between the rocks should extend at least 12" to 18" back into the bank providing a cool root run for the alpine plants. Avoid setting the rocks on end which tends to give a "jaws" or "tombstone" impression, and looks most unnatural. The rocks will hold warmth and moisture deep in the soil and insulate the plants from sudden changes of temperature.

Alpine Meadow Rockery:

Make sure your soil is really well-drained and construct a rolling contoured effect with low broad mounds of soil, large dog house sized rocks and a few shrubs. Use only very large rocks for focal points and flat rocks or gravel for pathways. Carpeting plants or ground covers (see Chapter 6) may be used instead of grass in low lying areas to connect mounds which are planted with alpines. This plan should provide a suitable environment for many plant preferences.

When all the rocks are securely positioned, the weeds have been controlled and the whole thing has settled over the winter, you are ready to begin planting. Try to make your rockery look as natural as possible. Use a variety of plants and do not regiment them in rows. Determine their ultimate expected spread and height. Plan blooming times so that there is always a point of interest in your rockery. Use dwarf shrubs and junipers for height and texture variation and evergreen effect. Do not neglect the smaller bulbs for spring colour. Low annuals are useful for filling gaps and providing bold splashes of bright colour. Stay away from any plant which will be too invasive and take over the whole thing. Provide coarse limestone grit (available from a feed store) for those plants which prefer alkaline conditions and dry surfaces. If you have sloped your rocks correctly your rockery should store sufficient water from the annual rainfall and snow melt but in times of severe drought you may water it deeply but gently. The rocks will act as a reservoir.

You may try any hardy plant which is short, spreading and likes well-drained conditions. The Alberta Horticulture Guide lists suitable perennials. Agriculture Canada has a pamphlet entitled *The Rock Garden* (Publication No. 1243, 1971). Both these publications are available through your District Agriculturist. To study a well-built and planted rockery, we recommend a visit to the Reader Rock Gardens in Calgary.

The following list recommends some easily grown and readily obtainable plants. There are many others with which the keen gardener may experiment.

Plants Suitable for Rock Gardens:

Perennials

Ajuga (Bugleweed)
Alyssum saxatile (Golden Alyssum)
Alpine Aster
Anemone patens (native prairie anemone, referred to as prairie crocus)
Artemesia (Silver Mound)
Arabis (Rock Cress - white)
Aubretia (Rock Cress - purple)
Bergenia
Campanula carpatica
Dianthus deltoides (Maiden Pinks)
Dianthus arenarius (Sand Pinks)
Dianthus plumaris (Hardy Pinks)
Dodecatheon (Shooting Star)
Festuca glauca (Blue Fescue)
Gentian - many kinds
Leontopodium (Edelweiss)
Myosotis (Forget-me-not)
Phlox borealis (Arctic Phlox)
Phlox subulata (Moss Phlox)
Saponaria (Soapwort)

Saxifrage (this wouldn't appear to be all that common!)
Sedum (Stonecrop - many kinds)
Sempervivum (Hens and Chicks - many kinds)
Thyme
Viola

Bulbs

Allium (any variety)
Chionodoxa (Glory of the Snow)
Iris reticulata
Muscari (Grape Hyacinth)
Scilla sibirica (Siberian Squill)
Tulip - dwarf varieties and species tulips.

Shrubs

Bird's Nest Spruce
Clavey's Dwarf Honeysuckle
Daphne cneorum (Rose Daphne)
Dwarf Juniper
Dwarf Mugho Pine
Pachistima (Cliff Greens)
Potentilla
Spirea froebelli

Plants Not Recommended for Rock Gardens (Too Invasive):

Aegopodium podograria (Goutweed)
Cerastium tomentosum (Snow in Summer)
Euphorbia cyparissias (Cypress Spurge)
Mint
Nepeta hederacea (Creeping Charlie)

Chapter Eleven

Flower

Arranging

Some Hints for Flower Arranging
by Patti Webb

When arranging flowers it is not necessary to rob the whole garden to make an arrangement. A few blooms can be made to go a long way, especially if the right containers and stem supports are used.

One of your first concerns when arranging fresh or dried flowers is what you are going to use for a container. The container need not be elaborate or expensive, in fact you may find that some of your best containers are found in the kitchen cupboard. Old tea pots, earthy coloured baking dishes or wine glasses can be used. Driftwood and sea shells make unique containers for dried materials.

Flowers can be dropped into a vase or container and left alone, but they will not look as attractive as when they are arranged in such a way that any unique quality such as a lovely curve, vivid colour or just the beauty of each bloom is clearly seen.

In order to position the stems in a definite design some means of support is necessary. Some supports that can be used are plastic foam (Oasis and Sahara blocks), pin holders and wire netting (chicken wire).

Plastic foam is the easiest support to use because it holds the stems

---

On Facing Page

Arrangements at Millarville Church Flower Festival

Top left: Calendulas make a showy Hogarth curve in a copper waterer.

Top right: Lythrum, petunias, asters and verbenas are attractive on a window sill.

Centre left: Another Flower Festival display.

Centre right: A miniature dried arrangement called "Grandma's Thimble".

Bottom right: Delphinium, Chrysanthemum, Shasta daisy and Cornflower (Centaurea cyanus)

Bottom left: On the old Church organ, yellow lilies, bronze dahlias, Shasta daisies and veronica.

exactly in place. It is sold in blocks which can be cut easily with a knife to whatever size is needed. The plastic foam called "Oasis" is used for fresh flowers because when the foam blocks are placed in water they absorb it. "Sahara" is used for supporting dried materials.

Pin holders consist of a lead base in which sharp vertical pins are embedded; shapes and sizes vary. Pin holders are very useful in shallow containers and are secured with florist clay.

Wire netting is cut into a desired size, crumpled up and pushed into a container. This support is sometimes more difficult to work in, but I find that the flowers stay fresh longer, mainly because there is nothing interfering with the water going up the stem.

Mechanics is a term used by flower arrangers for all the equipment which holds plant material in position. Since most mechanics are not very attractive they need to be hidden. This can easily be done with extra leaves or moss. Small pieces of driftwood, shells or stones are useful for concealment and they also add some interest.

After making your decision about a container and supports, choose your flowers and foliage. Cut only a few flowers and foliage when you begin, otherwise you will end up with an overcrowded arrangement. In order to have flowers and foliage last for any length of time after being cut you have to condition them properly. It takes some time and effort but it is worth it.

The best time to cut flowers or foliage is early in the morning or late evening. Have a bucket of warm water and a sharp knife with you. Cut the stem of the flower on a slant, remove any unnecessary foliage and place in the bucket of water. Stems which have not been put into water immediately should be recut removing 2" off the stem. Most flowers benefit from standing in deep water for a minimum of 2 hours. During this time it also helps if the bucket of water and flowers are put into a cool, dark place.

Stems vary in their structure which may be soft, hard and woody, hollow or milky. Each type requires a different preparation for conditioning so it can absorb as much water as possible to prevent wilting later.

Soft stems take in water easily and require no further preparations. However, cut down on the soaking period for spring, bulbous flowers because they tend to get soaked and floppy. Also they should be arranged in shallow water, e.g. tulips and daffodils.

Hard or woody stems have a thick protective covering which does not allow water in easily. About 2" of this covering should be peeled or scraped off. In addition to scraping, the ends should be smashed to expose more of the inner stem to the water - e.g. lilac, crabapple blossoms. An exception is the rose on which the stem is cut on as long a slant as possible.

Hollow stems are upended and filled with water and cotton batting is used to plug the end of the stem. The cotton acts as a wick. Filling of the stem prevents premature falling of the flowers, e.g. lupines, delphiniums.

A few stems contain a milky substance which when cut leaks out or bleeds. It then dries and forms a layer over the stem preventing it from taking up water. This can be prevented by holding the stem end in a flame until it stops sizzling and there isn't any sign of bleeding, e.g. poppies, dahlias, poinsettas.

Leaves also have to be conditioned. Since they can take in water through their outside surface without damage, they can be completely submerged in warm water for 2 hours or more. Don't submerge grey foliage as it will become water-logged and will appear green. Just place stem ends in the water, e.g. Dusty Miller.

There are a few guide lines to follow when arranging your flowers. The height of an arrangement can be determined by making the arrangements 1½ times the height of the container (a tall one) or 1½ times the width of a low one. The flowers at the top of your arrangement should be light in colour whereas the darker colours should be closer to the container to give a balanced effect. Place the tallest flower or branch in the centre and vary the heights of the other flowers or foliage around it. Try to create a triangle in the frame of your arrangement.

Everlastings
by Betty Nelson

Everlastings are mostly grown for dried arrangements. These, the most common, all need starting indoors in April and planting out around the first of June:

Helichrysum (**Strawflower**): comes in many colours. Gather the buds before they open, immediately cut the stem off flush with the back of the bud and insert floral wire. If you wait until they dry you can't get the wire in. The bud opens when it dries; small buds make small flowers and larger buds larger flowers. If the flower is open when picked it will dry out of shape. This is the only everlasting that can be washed. Dunk quickly in soapy water and then clear water. The flower will go back to the bud stage when wet but will open when hung to dry.

Helipterum (**Sunray or Acroclimium**): flowers are pink and white with a yellow centre. Pick in the bud or "just open" stage and hang to dry. These are rather delicate.

Limonium (**Statice or Sea Lavender**): comes in many colours. Let the bloom come well out before picking, then hang to dry.

Xeranthemum (**Immortelle**): colours are pink and purple. Pick in the bud or "just open" stage and hang to dry.

Lunaria (**Money plant or Honesty**): is a biennial like Sweet Rocket which blooms the second spring. The seed pods are silver membranes about one inch across. These seed pods are used in dried arrangements; sometimes the outer covering of the membrane has to be flicked off.

Echinops (**Globe Thistle**) and *Eryngium* (**Sea Holly**): are both perennials. You harvest the seed heads in the fall when they turn a metallic blue.

Other annuals worth trying are: Amaranthus (Love-lies-bleeding); Nigella (Love-in-a-mist) for its seed heads; Scabiosa (Starflower) for its seed heads.

Grasses: *Briza* (Quaking) and *Lagurus ovatus* (Hare's tail) are annuals. Pick before they get too ripe so they don't shatter.

Mixed packets of everlastings are usually annuals and produce some unusual plants. One, *Ammobium alatum,* is very nice. Pick the buds, hang to dry and they open into dainty little white stars.

Drying and Preserving Flowers and Foliage
by Patti Webb

There are numerous ways to preserve flowers and foliage for decorative uses and of these there are three methods I prefer to use as they are simple and very effective. They are the Hang Dry Method, the Sand Method and the Glycerine Method. Before describing these there are three important points to remember in gathering plants to be dried, no matter which method you use.

1. Select plants for drying at the best stage of development. Underdeveloped is preferable to overdeveloped.

2. Choose only fresh, perfect plants or flowers. Inferior quality will prove worthless.

3. Pick plants or flowers when their leaves, petals or other parts have the least amount of moisture content (i.e. noon on a sunny day - never after watering or a rain shower.)

Hang Dry Method
1. Gather plants, keeping in mind the three points mentioned above.
2. Remove excess foliage from plants. This lessens the bulk and speeds drying.
3. Group and bunch stems together and fasten bunches securely. Stems shrink in drying, therefore elastic ties are best.
4. Suspend bunches on a line or clothes hanger in a warm dry area with good circulation of air.

5. Dry for seven to ten days. If stems snap easily the plant is dry.
6. Remove dry plants. Do not dry longer than necessary. Store in a covered box until you want to use them.
7. Crushed material can sometimes be restored by steaming.

Examples of plants suitable for the hang dry method are Grasses, grains, foliage (large leaves), everlastings, heathers, herbs, seed pods on stalks, goldenrod and other similar plants.

Sand Method

Excellent results can be obtained with a much wider range of plants by using a little more complicated method. This requires burying the flowers or leaves in an absorbent substance used as a drying agent. This method not only draws out the moisture but keeps the original shape of the plant. There are a great many substances which can be used such as silica gel and borax mixtures, but I have found that clean, dry sand (not too coarse) works very well, plus it is far less expensive than the other substances.

1. Select a container of a suitable size to hold the flowers or leaves. It can be made of any material other than metal.
2. Sprinkle ½ inch of sand on the bottom of the container.
3. Gather flowers or plants for drying, keeping in mind the three important points mentioned at the beginning of the chapter.
4. Remove unnecessary parts and foliage.
5. Place flower on sand. It may be placed with head up or down, depending on its size and shape. A spike form may be laid lengthwise.
6. Sprinkle the sand in and about all parts of the flower. Make sure the flower is completely covered with sand.
7. Never cover the container during drying.
8. The time of drying depends on the size, texture and thickness of the flower. A week to ten days should be adequate.
9. Flowers are dry when stiff to touch.
10. Tilt the container to allow the sand to run from it and shake gently to remove sand.
11. Use an artist's camel hair brush to remove any sand particles on the petals.
12. If any petals come loose, glue them back in place and store dried flowers or leaves in a box until needed.
13. Stems may be replaced with wire and taped with florist's tape.

This is an excellent method for the so-called tender flowers such as roses, peonies, lilies, daffodils, tulips and all types of leaves.

There is a change in some colours as they dry. For example: red and purple turn darker; pink and blue remain fairly true to colour, white turns creamy-white. Scillas stay a true dark blue and Mockorange stays a true white. Yellow holds its true colour.

Glycerine Method

The glycerine treatment method is a very easy way to preserve mature foliage. The results are supple and not brittle as with the other two drying methods. However, the natural colours are not retained as with drying.

1. Pour into a jar one part glycerine and two parts very hot water and stir well.
2. Cut foliage which is in good condition and is at a mature stage but not old or beginning to dry. Young foliage does not take up moisture easily and usually wilts.
3. Place the stem ends in the glycerine and water mixture covering about two inches of the stem end. Placing the stems in the glycerine mixture while hot is helpful for rapid absorption.
4. Remove foliage when it has changed colour. As a rule the tougher the leaf the longer the time necessary.
5. Store preserved leaves in boxes in a dry place. Mildewing will occur if there is dampness present.
6. If glycerined foliage becomes dusty it can be washed in warm, soapy water and then rinsed. After rinsing shake excess water off and hang up until all water has evaporated.

Notes

Chapter Twelve

Vegetables, Herbs and Fruit

Section A — Vegetables

Ideally your vegetable garden should be located in a sheltered area where there is the most available sunlight and good drainage. A deep, rich soil which is neither too light nor too heavy is best for most vegetables. Well-rotted barnyard manure applied in the fall not only replenishes soil nutrients but improves soil texture as well. It can also be applied in the spring along with compost and should be worked into your garden either by digging with a spade or rototilling. Most gardeners in our area rototill two or three times in the spring and then rake the soil evenly in preparation for planting.

Squaring off your vegetable garden gives it a neat, tidy appearance and adds to the overall effect of your home gardens. To mark off your vegetable rows use a garden line which can easily be made by tying an appropriate length of strong twine to two stakes. Insert a stake at one end of your row, then run the twine the length of your row and insert your second stake at the other end, keeping the twine taut. Using the twine as your guide, hoe in your trench. Some gardeners recommend soaking each trench before planting your seed as this may aid in faster germination. If possible run your rows in a north/south direction planting your shortest plants (i.e. carrots, radish) on the east side of the garden. By arranging your garden in this manner your plants will receive full sun on three sides. If your garden is on a north or south slope, rows should run from east to west to retain moisture and prevent soil erosion.

It is a good idea to make a gardening notebook for yourself in which

On Facing Page
Top: A rural vegetable garden offers a bountiful harvest.
Bottom left: Rescue Apple-crab, one of the hardiest.
Bottom right: Raspberries.

you can make annual notations about the types and varieties of vegetables you grew, the success you had, when and how you planted them, and so forth. Keeping a record of what you planted in each row of your garden (best done by numbering the rows) will assist you in crop rotation. This process involves moving your root, top, and leaf crops to a different location in the garden every year which greatly helps in disease prevention.

Your garden soil needs to warm up before you plant most of your vegetable seeds. Cold soil can retard germination and growth. If you plan to mulch your garden to retain moisture and keep down weeds, wait until early July when the soil has had a chance to get warm. For mulch you can use peat moss, compost, lawn clippings, sawdust, hay, well-rotted barnyard manure or clean straw. To be effective it should be put on in a layer several inches thick. In the fall it is simply dug into the soil. Black plastic has also been used as a mulch by some gardeners. It not only conserves moisture and keeps down weeds, but it helps retain heat as well. Not everyone uses a mulch. It is something each gardener can experiment with to see if it is of advantage to him or not.

If you don't use one of the above mulches, hoe and rake after each rain or watering as soon as the soil is dry on top. This is known as dust mulching which is just plain good farming. It will keep down the weeds and conserve moisture.

In most cases it is best to water your vegetable garden in the morning before the sun gets too hot. Try to avoid watering in the evening. A long, deep soaking is much better for your garden than frequent sprinklings, and if at all possible try to water with warmish water. Ponds and dugouts are a good source of water. It is a warmer temperature than well water and contains many organic nutrients. It is also naturally soft water which is better for your plants. If soil and slope conditions permit we recommend trickle irrigation as the best method of watering.

Rain barrels to catch the rain water from roofs are a must. This is the best water for your plants, inside or out. Water conservation should be the main concern of every gardener. Surface watering rather than overhead sprinkling should be practised where possible. The water table is having more holes drilled into it every day, and the supply below ground is not inexhaustible.

When it comes time to thin your vegetable rows (when seedlings are about two inches high) try to do so when the soil is damp. Be sure to firm your soil down well after thinning.

Recommended Vegetables and Varieties
Even though we live in an area where late and early frosts are a frustrating reality, a number of vegetables are grown successfully. These are listed below. All the varieties mentioned in this chapter have been

tried and proven successful. However, bear in mind that new and improved hybrids are being developed all the time so you should refer to your Alberta Horticultural Guide each year.

Beans:

Bush Type (Green) - *Blue Lake; Tendergreen; Dwarf Stringless*
Bush Type (Yellow) - *Golden Wax*

If the soil is warm you can sow beans in mid-May. Cover on cold nights. Very susceptible to frost. Don't cultivate or disturb beans when wet. In low-lying areas near the mountains it is difficult to grow beans due to frost. Harvest when beans break easily when snapped. In fall, after frost, cut off tops leaving roots in ground as they provide nitrogen.

Storage: blanch and freeze; can.

Broad Beans:

Broad Windsor

Plant early as they are slow growing. Quite hardy - will withstand spring frost. Pinch out growing top when plants are about 30" high or when they have 4 or 5 sprays of flowers.

Storage: pick when young and tender to blanch and freeze.

Pole Beans:

Scarlet Runner

Sensitive to frost - must be grown with protection either against a wall or fence. Attract hummingbirds.

Storage: blanch and freeze.

Beets:

Tendersweet; Detroit Dark Red; Formanova; Early Wonder

When harvesting beets, twist tops off to prevent bleeding rather than cutting. Beet greens are very high in vitamins - they can be harvested when young and cooked like spinach.

Storage: Pickle; cook and freeze.

Broccoli:

Green Comet; Green Duke; Di Cicco; Cleopatra

Start indoors under lights or in the greenhouse in mid-April. Harden off in cold frame as early as possible. After transplanting in garden put a tin can from which both ends have been removed around seedling and push down in soil about 2". Remove before plant gets too big. This protects plant from wind and cutworms. Likes manure and well-watered rich soil. Harvest centre head first when still hard and green. Take 3" to 4" of stem with flower head to produce high yield on side shoots.

Storage: blanch and freeze.

Brussels Sprouts:

Jade Cross Hybrid F1; Half Dwarf.

Same procedure as for broccoli. To hasten development, remove growing point when first sprouts are firm and remove lower leaves as sprouts form. Pick lower sprouts first. Require long, cool growing season. Harvest in late September.

Storage: blanch and freeze.

Cabbage:
Red - *Red Head;* Savoy - *Chieftan Drumhead.*

Early cabbage: *Golden Acre* or *Early Marvel* have a small, firm, round head which matures in early July. Mid-season varieties such as *Bonanza* cabbage are a general purpose cabbage which can be used for coleslaw, etc. For storage purposes you should grow a late season cabbage such as *Danish Ballhead* or *Ultragreen. Red Cabbage* is grown for salads and pickling as well as for its ornamental effect.

Storage: Blanch and freeze; store in cold room; pickle; make sauerkraut.

Carrots:
Amsterdam; Nantes Strong Top; Early Cross Hybrid F1; Imperator; Touchon; Chantenay Types.

Gourmet Carrots - *Parisienne* (harvest when young) like a sandy soil. Sow in garden in May. Water regularly - too much or too little water causes problems. To prevent green shoulders keep roots covered with soil. Plant in rows the width of your hoe and sprinkle seed randomly down the trench. This helps carrots to come up and although not much more space is used than if you planted a thin row, your yield is much greater. Harvest before heavy frost. Thin by using young carrots early in the season. Carrots for fall harvest must have room to grow.

Storage: Cut ½" down from the crown to prevent growth and store in sand in cold room or in plastic bags in 'fridge; blanch and freeze; dry; pickle.

Cauliflower:
Self-Blanche (this variety doesn't need to be tied up); *Super Snowball; Early Snowball; Igloo.*

Same procedure as for broccoli. As soon as head becomes visible tie the leaves loosely up around the plant to prevent yellowing. Cauliflower requires a great deal of water so keep soil moist. Cold nights after planting out causes blind heads (no head at all). Plant out later than broccoli and cabbage.

Storage: Blanch and freeze at their prime; dry.

Celery:
Utah Green; Golden Crisp; Self-blanching

Start indoors under lights or in the greenhouse in mid-March. Plant in garden after danger of frost is past in 10" deep trench which is filled in as celery grows. Needs lots of water and likes rich soil. Cold nights can cause bolting. Utah Green tolerates cold weather.

Storage: Blanch and freeze in unsalted water; dry.

Corn:
Amazing Early Alberta; Alberta Gold; Spancross; Polar Vee; Earlivee.

Likes lots of sun and rich, light loam. Must be sheltered from the wind. Needs constant water at silk stage. Plant 3 or 4 rows together with a distance of 3' between rows for pollination. Most sweet corn will not germinate at soil temperatures under 50°F so it cannot be sown in your garden until your soil has warmed sufficiently which may mean early June. Cover on cold nights after growing point comes up for it is very sensitive to frost. Pick corn when silk on cobs is brown and dry and kernels are well formed.

Storage: Blanch and freeze on or off the cob; dry.

Kohlrabi:
Early Purple; Early White.

Start indoors or sow seed directly in garden. Freezes well.

Storage: Blanch and freeze.

Leeks:
Large American Flag; Titan.

Start the same way as onions and hill them as they grow.

Storage: Blanch and freeze.

Lettuce:
Head - Iceberg; Great Lakes; New York; Tom Thumb
Butterhead - Buttercrunch
Cos - Cosmo
Leaf - Grand Rapids; Ruby Red

Sow seed thinly in early May. When 2'' high thin to 12'' apart. Thinnings may be transplanted. Water with trickle irrigation. Doesn't like hot weather. Can make successive plantings for continuous crop. Slugs can be a problem.

Storage: Dill as cucumbers.

Onions:
Autumn Spice; Sweet Spanish Utah Strain; Yellow Globe Danvers; Canada Maple; Fiesta
Pickling Onions - *White Port Silverskins.*

Start indoors or in the greenhouse - the later you plant them the hotter the flavour. As they grow add more soil and feed instead of pricking out. Near the end of May, immerse flat in water so that seedlings can be easily pulled apart. Plant 4'' apart in a 3'' deep trench. In August, remove soil from the top half of the onion and bend the tops over - this assists in the ripening process. At the first sign of frost remove onions from the garden. Set out in sunny location every day to dry on a screen

Braided Onions

for air circulation. When tops shrivel up they are dry. Hang in a dry place in old nylon stockings or net bags.

Storage: Dry; braid and hang in dry place; freeze (no need to blanch).

Parsnips:
Improved Hollow Crown

Slow to germinate so sow radish seed with it to mark the row. Deep soil preparation is a must. Light frost improves the flavour. Leave some in the ground all winter and dig as soon as the soil thaws in the spring. Thin to give growing space.

Storage: Blanch and freeze; dry.

Peas:
Little Marvel; Homesteader; Laxton's Progress; Freezer 69.
Edible Pod Peas - *Sugar Snap.*

As soon as your vegetable garden is dry enough to work, plant at least 1 row of peas. Plant varieties with different maturing dates for a continuous supply of fresh, young peas all summer. Often peas are planted 2 rows at a time, the rows being 6'' to 8'' apart. In the space between the rows put in support posts every 3' or 4' and stretch 1'' chicken wire between them. Your peas will climb on and be supported by this wire and harvesting will be much easier. Peas like moist, rich earth so do not let your soil dry out. To avoid powdery mildew, remove old, unproductive plants by pruning at ground level. If your plants are attacked by powdery mildew be sure to remove and burn all the infected plants - don't put them in the compost heap. Roots of plants are left in the ground as they are full of nitrogen.

Storage: Blanch and freeze; dry.

Potatoes:
Kennebec; Warba; Norland; Netted Gem; Irish Cobbler

Help to clean the soil of weeds by competition and they break up the soil. Potatoes use a lot of soil nutrients which must be replenished the following year. Like a well-drained loam. Avoid letting the ground dry out or get too wet. Plant potatoes in rows which are 3' apart with plants 18'' apart in the row. When they break through the soil, build the earth up around them. As they grow continue to do this to support the stems and to keep the sun from the tubers. This process is called "hilling". It is best to harvest potatoes on an overcast day. Spread potatoes on a dry, flat surface to dry out, leaving some dirt on them. As soon as they are dry (a few hours) put in a humid, cool spot which is completely dark, for exposure to light causes their surface to turn green and poisonous. Potatoes keep well in bushel baskets in the cold room.

Storage: As above.

Pumpkin:
Spirit

Grow the same as squash - needs lots of space and lots of heat.

Storage: On a shelf in cold room or root cellar.

Radishes:
Early Scarlet Globe; Cherry Belle; French Breakfast; White Icicle.

May be planted every 10 days for continuous supply from early May on. Mix with rows of lettuce and carrots which assists in their germination. Otherwise plant in blocks 2' or 3' square. Flea beetles can destroy radishes - to repel beetles plant mint with radishes or spray with catnip tea. Maggots can be controlled by spreading crushed egg shells over the soil surface around the plants. Grow best in cool weather so plant in spring.

Storage: Winter radish can be stored in cold room or root cellar.

Rutabaga: (Swede Turnip)
Altasweet; Laurentian.

These are grown for winter storage. Sow outdoors at the end of May. Must be thinned to 10'' apart. Water and cultivate regularly. Root maggots and flea beetles are a problem. In the fall when harvested, paint with a thin layer of melted parafin wax after removing all maggot holes, then store in the cold room. Or put in plastic bags, leave the tops open and store in the cold room.

Storage: As above. Also can blanch and freeze or cook, mash and freeze; dry.

Spinach:
King of Denmark; Hybrid #7 F1; Leaf Beet Perpetual Spinach; Long Standing Bloomsdale.

Sow seed in garden in early May. Water frequently. Likes well-rotted manure and rich soil. Keep cut so it keeps producing and doesn't bolt. Leaf Beet Perpetual Spinach will not bolt.

Storage: blanch and freeze. Cook in larger quantities and freeze in family size servings, undrained.

Squash:
Zucchini Summer Squash - *Zucchini Select; Gold Rush.*

Start indoors in peat pots and transplant to warm, protected spot which has lots of sun or start outdoors under hot caps. Likes well-rotted manure or manure tea. When fruit starts to develop pick flower off end of fruit and discard. Young fruit is generally best. Very susceptible to frost. Zucchini is the fastest growing squash.

Storage: Pickle; Dry; Freeze; Grate and freeze for later use in baking.

Summer Scallop Squash - *St. Pat.* Grow as Above.

Vegetable Spaghetti Squash - Grow in cold frame.

Buttercup Squash - *Sweet Mama.* Grow in cold frame.

Swiss Chard:
Silver Giant; Ruby Red; Fort Hope Giant.

Plant end of May. Water frequently. Both stem and leaves are edible.

Storage: Blanch and freeze; dill; make relish.

Tomatoes:
Sub Arctic; Starfire; Rocket; Brookpact.

Should be started indoors. Like rich well-drained soil. Fertilize with manure tea. Prune a number of the shoots from the axils of the leaves and in mid-summer pinch off any blossoms as there is not time for them to produce fruit. You want to concentrate the plant's energy on developing and maturing existing fruit. Must be grown in a warm, sheltered spot or in a cold frame. To prevent blossom end rot, an even supply of water is essential. Tomatoes are pollinated by the wind, not bees. When planted in greenhouse shake plant at mid-day to assure pollination and proper fruit formation. Variety maturity days mentioned in catalogues refer to the number of days from setting of blossom to the ripening of the fruit. Don't grow anything with a longer day length than 56 days.

Storage: Blanch, peel, stew and freeze; puree raw in blender, put in containers (e.g. empty yogurt cups) and freeze; can; make juice; dry.

126

Turnip:
Purple Top White Globe.
  Not a storage turnip. Same growing directions as Rutabaga.

Section B

Herbs
by Patti Webb

  Since I have started growing herbs I have found it a fascinating and rewarding part of gardening. Herbs can be grown along with your vegetables and flowers or you can plant them in a special spot of their own. Some of them can also be potted up and kept indoors to use during the winter. Most herbs grow well in a protected area in full sun.

  I would like to share with you some of the experiences I have had growing and using herbs.

  Pick leaves and flowers when flower buds are about half open - they have the most flavour and aroma at this stage. Also pick before noon, as soon as the sun has dried off the dew. Try not to crush them, as they will lose their fragrance, and do not gather more herbs than you can deal with quickly. It is, of course, better to use fresh herbs when possible but this is not always practical so we have to preserve them in some manner for future use.

Air Drying

Method 1 - all herbs should be dried in an airy, dry, darkened place
          - cut herbs with a sharp knife
          - tie into bunches and hang upside down
          - should be dry in 2-3 weeks
          - ready when brittle to touch

Method 2 - faster method
          - spread wet herbs on newspaper, cotton, cheesecloth, or non-metallic mesh and arrange so air can circulate around them.
          - drying area should be warm and dry (can use food dryer)
          - check herbs after about 12 hours - if they are brittle to touch they are ready to be stored.

Storing
- strip leaves from stems
- do not crumble too much or they lose their flavour
- crumble or pulverize just before using for best flavour and aroma
- put into clean airtight containers
- label and date containers (after a year discard old herbs)
- keep jars in dark part of the kitchen

Freezing
- herbs are quickly and easily frozen
- gather herbs, wash and shake off any water
- put into plastic bags, label, date and freeze

Note : Flavour in dried herbs is more concentrated than in fresh or frozen, so you need a smaller amount. Usually ⅓ to ½ the amount you would use of fresh or frozen herbs.

The following are herbs I have grown and used:

Chives:
- use fresh, frozen or dried.
- use where a mild onion flavour is needed

Lemon Balm:
- use fresh or dried
- makes excellent tea
- use in potpourri and herb bath

Borage:
- use fresh or dried
- use in salads
- makes good tea and fruit drinks
- flowers can be used to decorate salads or fish dishes
- flowers and leaves can be used in potpourri

Dandelion:
- use fresh
- very nutritious
- use leaves in salads
- flowers are used to make wine

Dill:
- use fresh or dried
- cut dill heads as soon as flower buds form
- for milder flavour snip off green sprigs
- dill seed can be gathered when they turn brown just before pods burst
- use both leaves and seeds to flavour vinegar
- add to bland vegetables, salads, herb breads and fish dishes
- chewing dill seeds will freshen you breath

Garlic:
- use fresh or dried
- store the bulbs like onions
- I found our growing season wasn't long enough for them to mature properly- you can try starting them indoors and then plant out in a warm, protected location. Leave some in garden for next spring's use.

- for drying, peel and chop garlic bulbs and dry
- put dried pieces into blender and grind into fine powder
- uses: we enjoy the flavour of garlic, so I use it in most of my main dishes.
- reputed to repel gophers.

Marjoram:
- fresh or dried
- uses: sprinkle over lamb or beef before roasting, use in potpourri

Mint:
- fresh or dried
- use when cooking lamb
- makes excellent jelly and sauce
- use fresh leaves in salads or chopped with early vegetables
- makes excellent tea
- fresh leaves make refreshing garnishes on beverages and main dishes
- mint added to bath water is supposed to help itchy skin
- plant in a contained area or it will get away on you, e.g. a bottomless five-gallon pail.

Parsley:
- use fresh or dried
- there is practically no dish it will not improve
- when used as a garnish it makes any dish look more tempting
- makes a good tea
- counteracts bad breath or the odor of garlic

Rosemary:
- use fresh or dried
- pick young tender leaves as soon as their aroma has developed
- do not wash
- use with lamb dishes
- use in potpourri
- many be kept over winter as a houseplant

Sage:
- use fresh or dried
- do not wash leaves
- has a very strong flavour so use sparingly
- is good with all rich, fatty meats
- important ingredient in bread stuffings
- makes a good spring tonic tea

Summer Savory:
- use fresh or dried
- do not wash leaves

- increases flavour in all bean dishes
- use in stuffings
- use fresh in salads

Thyme:
- use fresh or dried
- do not wash
- has a very strong flavour so use sparingly
- can be used in all meat and cheese dishes
- used for tea
- use in potpourri
- use in bath for tired, aching muscles

Herb Tea

Whatever your taste buds desire in flavour will determine what herb or combination or herbs you will use for your herb tea. Just about every herb can be used for tea. All teas are made in the normal way. Just warm the pot, put in the herbs, pour in boiling water and allow to steep for 5-10 minutes. 1 teaspoon of dried herbs for each cup and one for the pot, or, if you use fresh herbs use 3 teaspoons per cup.

Herbs in the Bath

Herbs added to a bath are refreshing and fragrant. Just add fresh leaves or flowers to the bath water or you can put them into a bag and hang under the hot water tap. You may also make a strong herb tea and add it to the bath water. The following herbs can be used: thyme, mint, lemon balm and dandelion.

Herb Potpourri

The sweet fresh scent of summer can be captured all year round in potpourri. It is easy to make and makes a nice gift. It is used to scent drawers and cupboards and it helps keep moths away.

The following herbs and flowers can be used: lemon balm, borage, thyme, marjoram, mint, sage, rosemary, wild rose petals and clover.

Make sure all flowers and leaves are dried well before making potpourri. Extra scent can be added by mixing in spices such as cloves, nutmeg and cinnamon. Mix thoroughly and put into a suitable covered container or make into sachets for drawers or closets.

Herb Pillows

Make a small pillow out of scraps of fabric. Fill the pillows with dried herbs and stitch shut. If put under your pillow or behind your neck when going to bed it is supposed to help induce sleep, plus it gives off a pleasant aroma. Herbs most often used for pillows are dill, lemon balm, marjoram, sage and thyme.

Perennial Herbs and Vegetables
Asparagus:

This perennial vegetable takes 4 years from seed to be edible. Otherwise transplant 2 year old plants purchased from a nursery. Need deep, rich well prepared soil. Fertilize in April with a high nitrogen fertilizer before it starts to grow. Needs lots of water. Harvest spears until the middle of June. Female plants bear berries so dig up and throw away as they don't produce as well as male plants.

Storage: Best to eat fresh. Asparagus enthusiasts have the water boiling before they even go out and cut it.

Chives:

A perennial herb which likes full sun. Produces onion-like greens in the early spring which have a lovely flavour. Can divide plant in spring or fall.

Storage: Freeze; dry.

Horseradish:

This perennial vegetable spreads rapidly so you should plant in a separate bed. Can harvest roots 2 years after planting. Harvest roots early.

Storage: Make into sauce.

Mint:

A perennial herb which likes semi-shade and moist soil. Bad for spreading.

Storage: Freeze; make jelly; dry for tea.

Rhubarb:

Is a perennial vegetable which prefers rich, well-drained, deeply worked soil and a sunny location. Plant roots just below the soil surface in May and allow to grow for two years before harvesting stalks. When seed stalks form, cut them off near the ground. To force a rhubarb plant for early eating encircle with bucket from which the bottom has been removed or else with several rubber tires. Remove later in the season. For jelly recipes calling for lemon juice, use rhubarb juice.

Storage: Jam; jelly; freeze; make juice, relish or chutneys; wine; dry, use in pies and other desserts.

Section C — Fruit
Apples:

Growing apples in this region is definitely a challenge! However, when you harvest the first pail of apples off your own trees you will decide it was really worth the effort.

There are a few tricks to achieving success with your orchard. The first is to choose varieties that are hardy enough to withstand our climate. The second is to plant them where they get some shelter from prevailing winds. A good snow cover is a help in keeping the roots frozen. Mulching after freeze-up with leaves and clippings helps, too. Be sure they are well watered-in late in the fall.

Now, what varieties can we grow? Crabapples are the hardiest. There are lovely flowering ones, such as *Hopa* and *Royalty,* grown mainly for their blooms; their apples are small and hard. The birds love them though. Others such as *Dolgo* produce bigger apples good for jelly making.

Then there are applecrabs which are a cross between crabs and regular apples. *Rescue* is one of the best, a vigorous grower which produces when quite young.

If you want to try real apples here are a few to try:

Early:
Heyer 12 - good cooking green apple, does not keep long
Norland - a new one in 1981. Has better keeping qualities than Heyer 12

Mid-season:
Battleford - worth a try
Patterson - worth a try
Sunnybrook (new in 1982) - worth a try

Consult your Alberta Horticultural Guide for recommended varieties each year. New ones are continually being developed.

Currants
by Theresa Patterson

No garden is complete without a few currant bushes, red, white or black or all three. The black ones have a strong pungent flavour, delicious in jam or jelly. Old-time remedies for colds recommend black currant juice in hot water, also good on a cold winter night even if you don't have a cold. Red and white currants make superb jelly. Their seediness does not make nice jam. Added to other fruits such as raspberries, gooseberries or crabapples they make jellies of excellent flavour.

It is best to provide your currant bushes with a permanent home where you can keep them free of weeds and grass. They will produce for many years. Whatever kind of soil you have it should be dug deeply and enriched with manure before planting. You can buy two-year old plants or get some from neighbours by layering the lower branches or by taking cuttings.

Red and white currants are very susceptible to aphids and spider mites which will denude your bushes of leaves if not treated. The crop will suffer as a result. Black currants do not seem to be affected as badly, perhaps because of their pungent odour.

It is important to prune currants to get a good crop of berries.

Excellent instructions on growing currants can be found in the publication *Bush Fruits in Alberta,* Fact Sheet #230/-2 which is available from your District Agriculturalist.

Raspberries
by Theresa Patterson

Raspberries are a prolific fruit crop, well worth the little extra care they require to be successful in this chinook area. Since they bear fruit only on new canes from the previous year, the problem is how to bring those canes through the winter. Location also has a bearing on how well they will survive. An ideal location is an east-west row on the north side of a row of poplar trees. Leave at least twenty feet of space between the trees and the raspberries to allow for cultivation. Also the trees will steal moisture from the raspberries. Avoid full sun and lack of protection.

Raspberries do well in black soil or lighter if well manured and mulched with straw or hay. The mulch conserves moisture and keeps out weeds and grass. Do not cultivate too close to the row or it encourages excessive suckering. Keep the row to no more than two plants in width. Remove extra suckers. It takes 3 or 4 years to establish a row that produces heavily.

They require ample amounts of water from flowering season right through fruiting. A plastic pipe with holes drilled every 5 or 6 inches which can be attached to a garden hose works well. Run the pipe down the middle of the row and leave it there all summer. Soak thoroughly as needed.

In late October or just before freeze-up bend the canes in a curve, using a light pole, until the tips touch the ground. Then place a board on the tips and shovel enough soil on it to hold the tips securely down. Be careful not to break them where they leave the ground. The snow will drift over them and protect them from the drying effect of the chinook winds. They do not require covering with straw or hay.

In the spring when the trees are beginning to leaf out, it is time to let the raspberries up. Uncover the tips and shake off the dirt. Now is the time to thin out the old canes that bore fruit last year. They will not have any new leaves coming. They look dry and lighter in colour than the new canes. Also thin out some of the new canes, leaving no more than 4 or 5 to a plant. The tops should also be cut back to no more than shoulder height. This encourages side shoots that produce fruit. Canes that grow 6 or 7 feet high are hard to pick, they dry out and fall over. The canes need tying up now too. Posts located every 10 or 15 feet down the row lend support. Strong baler twine run from post to post on each side of the row gives good support if cross ties are put in to separate the canes. Time spent in careful tying pays off at picking time.

Find a variety that thrives in your neighbourhood from a local source rather than ordering from elsewhere. Success is assured!

Everbearing Strawberries
by Norma Lyall

I have tried six kinds of strawberries in the last eight years and find the everbearing is the best variety for our climate and soil. This variety does well in almost any kind of soil, the berries are red all the way through and you will have two crops of berries a year, in July and September depending on the weather.

When planting strawberries you should have a place worked up the year before planting. You could work in natural fertilizer and old straw if you have clay soil. Try to kill all the weeds. If you don't have a place worked up the first year try your luck anyway and start another patch the next year from the runners that grew from this year's plants. Once you have a few strawberry plants you will always have them for I don't think they would all winter kill.

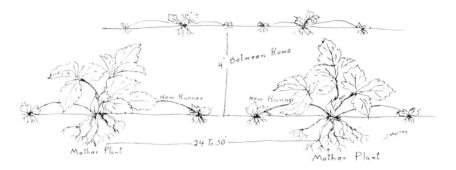

As I have lots of garden space I plant my plants 24" to 30" apart in the row and between the rows I leave 4'. For those who haven't got much space put plants 14" apart in the row and 36" between rows. I like to plant my strawberries like the diagram above so I can just leave 2 runners of each plant in between the mother plant. This saves transplanting. Once runners start you should go out every few days and place them where you want them to grow, cutting off the ones you don't want. You should only let about 4 to 6 runners grow from the mother plant each year. I let them bear fruit the first year as it is so much work to keep the flowers cut off. Remember not to hoe deeply around the plants because the roots spread out and are just below the surface. You should plant some new plants each year removing 3 or 4 year old plants which are not doing very well.

Strawberries do best if there is a nice warm rain once a week and the weather is hot. Everything likes this kind of weather. Because of their shallow roots they should be kept moist but don't allow standing water.

As strawberries catch all the weed seeds that blow around such as dandelions and thistles which thrive around the plants, they are very hard to manage. At times looking after runners and weeds keeps one busy all summer, but the berries are worth the work you put into them. Also when you have visitors all you need to do is take them out to the garden to the strawberry patch and tell them to eat as many as they like, *then* invite them in for tea. Sure handy when you haven't any cookies baked.

We have another problem in this part of the world which is winter kill. This occurs when we have a mild winter and not much snow. One fall before freeze up we covered the plants with old straw in which the weed seeds had sprouted and died. I left it to rot between the rows which kept the moisture in and the weeds down and also helped to keep the dirt off the berries. When the trees start to bud you should take this straw off the plants a little each day and let the heat from the sun warm the plants. It might be late April or May when you uncover as no year is the same. This old straw prevented winter kill however the dear little mice got into it and subsequently ate some of the strawberry plants off at the roots. Since then we have used old sawdust or old shavings as a winter cover which has worked well. We uncover them the same way and leave the old shavings between the plants and the rows.

Strawberries must be planted with the crown of the plant level with the surface of the soil. If the crown is buried the plant will have difficulty growing and if the crown is above the surface the roots will dry out.

 **Helpful Hints**

To store carrots over winter:
   a.   *cut off enough of the carrot to remove growing part - they won't sprout and grow in storage.*
   b.   *store in layers separated by newspaper in styrofoam coolers with lid closed.*
   c.   *store in cardboard boxes with lid closed.*
   d.   *store in pails covered with plastic bags.*
   e.   *store in moist sand or peat moss. Do not allow the mix to become too dry.*

When planting out cabbage family plants and onions prune leaves back halfway, especially if temperature is high. It cuts down on evaporation, prevents wilting and plant shock and gives roots time to get established.

Throw in a few radish seeds when you plant slow germinating seeds like parsnips, parsley, carrots and asparagus seed. It helps you find the rows when doing your first weeding.

Chapter Thirteen

Greenhouses

by Anne Vale

To have your own greenhouse is the ambition of every serious gardener. When British Columbia gardeners are rejoicing in their springtime and enticing us with news of daffodils and forsythia in bloom those thumbs start to itch to begin growing. When you dig your way out to the greenhouse on a snowy March morning there is nothing like the smell of the green freshness of growing things which greets you when you open the door on your own patch of spring.

It doesn't have to be a very expensive and elaborate greenhouse. A simple structure of old storm windows with a fibreglass roof, or a row of steel arches covered with polythene will grow plants which are just as good as those grown in a glass and aluminum greenhouse with all the gadgets. Even without extra heat it is possible to extend the growing season a month at either end and attempt the growing of vegetables not normally possible because they cannot tolerate our cold nights.

You will be able to start you own bedding plants and vegetable transplants, and also grow an amazing quantity of tomatoes, cucumbers, squashes, etc. Usually it gets too cold and dark by the end of October to ripen tomatoes successfully, but there are always pet plants looking for a cool winter home and others which can be grown in a cool greenhouse run at 55° - 60°F (12-15°C) all winter. Fuchsia, primula, azaleas, spring bulbs and lots more ornamentals will grow and bloom happily at these temperatures.

The greenhouse should be located with sunlight in mind. If you are going to start seeds and grow tomatoes and cucumbers or operate it year

---

On Facing Page

Top: Wood and coal stove does the heating.

Lower: A hobby greenhouse need not be elaborate.

round you are going to need every minute of available sunlight in winter and early spring. We are so far north that our winter hours of darkness severely reduce the growth of plants until after the spring equinox. If your greenhouse is shaded for even part of the day in winter or early spring all you will be able to grow is plants with a low light requirement. It is much easier to shade the greenhouse from too much light later in summer than to create extra light when you really need it.

When considering the size of your greenhouse remember that the smaller the bubble of air you have captured the quicker will it change temperature every time the sun goes behind a cloud. If you cannot be there all the time to open and shut windows and doors, it is a good investment to purchase some automatic ventilating equipment which will take care of temperature extremes for you.

In an attached lean-to greenhouse on the south side of a building obviously there is a solid north wall insulated by the warmth of the attached building. This is a great help to your fuel bills. In a free-standing greenhouse it is better to orient it from north to south so that the sun travels around and shines on it from each side. The north wall can then be fully insulated and also the sides up to bench height and down a foot into the ground should be insulated with styrofoam. This too goes a long way to help with your fuel economy. Remember also that the winds can play havoc with anything not securely anchored and create a wind chill factor which can mean severe heat loss. Fences and hedges far enough away to provide shelter without shading can be of great benefit.

A lot of work is being done on solar greenhouses but they have a long way to go before they are an economic proposition. Actually all greenhouses to some extent are solar greenhouses in that they trap and increase the heat of the sun's rays. Forty-five gallon drums, filled with water, and painted black on the side facing the sun, white on the greenhouse side and placed on the sunny side of the greenhouse under the bench, will absorb the sun's heat during the day and store the heat in the water to be radiated into the greenhouse at night. The soil and the plants themselves absorb the heat from the sun and radiate it out again at night, and condensation on the inside of the greenhouse's covering reflects the infra-red rays back down to the plants again.

Infra-red heaters are the coming thing in greenhouse heating. Other alternatives are natural gas or propane heaters, either of which should be vented to the outside. Conventional electric heaters are too expensive and not capable of producing sufficient reserve b.t.u.'s to cope with a sudden plunge in the outdoor temperature.

Even if you only run your greenhouse from the first of March to mid October this will be time enough to grow some of the longer season annuals like pansies, lobelia and snapdragons and to have them blooming by the beginning of July. You can then follow the spring seedlings with a respectable crop of tomatoes and cucumbers.

References:

see Chapter on Annuals, seed sowing section.

Greenhouse Grow How by John H. Pierce. Published by Plants Alive Books, Seattle, U.S.A. Gives complete and detailed structural and cultural information. This book is a valuable text book for anyone building or operating a greenhouse of any size, and in any climate.

Hobby Greenhouse in Alberta by the Alberta Department of Agriculture. Available from your District Agriculturalist, Publication #Agdex 731-5.

 **Helpful Hints**

To stop leaks in your wooden rain barrel put in horse bran or porridge oats. Save all the rainwater you can. It's good for your houseplants.

To avoid cutting tomato plants, tie stalks to support stakes with pantyhose that have been cut lengthwise.

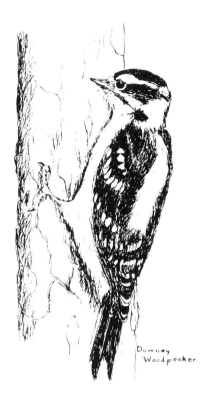

Downey
Woodpecker

Chapter Fourteen

Birds

Nature's Bug Catchers
by Janet MacKay

Among the most rewarding and useful things that you can raise in your garden are young birds. They're fascinating to watch, delightful to listen to and are useful in keeping down insects. There are many ways to attract the different kinds to one's yard.

In the wintertime a strategically placed feeder will bring the chickadees in by the dozens. The mixed bird seed sold in stores isn't the best thing to put in it. They won't eat the millet and other seeds like that. They just throw them aside to get at the sunflower seeds and the peanuts that are in these mixtures. I put oatmeal in mine and they really like that. They love sunflower seeds but my birds just get them for a treat each day. With so many around, a feeder-full wouldn't last long. I find if they get one that is a bit tough they drop it and get a new one. I have a storm window that has the holes in it so I just slide pill bottles in there with the seeds in them. When the seeds are gone they will rap on a pill bottle to let me know they would like some more. They likely know I'm pretty soft hearted.

You might wonder what good they are doing in the garden if they have a steady handout. But they spread out from the feeder and are busy

---

On Facing Page
Top: A winter project, new bird houses ready for early spring placement.
Centre left: White Crowned Sparrow.
Centre right: Black Capped Chickadee.
Lower left: Yellow Warbler.
Lower right: House Wren.

all day coming and going. In my yard there are a lot of big spruce trees and they are full of chickadees all day. A great many bugs, including aphids, lay their eggs on the branches in the fall. Every branch and twig on the trees is examined hundreds of times by the birds during the long winter, and I'm sure they don't miss much.

Hermit Thrush

I also hang fat in an onion bag for the chickadees and woodpeckers. There are two kinds of woodpeckers - the Hairy, which is black and white, with the male having a red spot on the back of his head, and the Downey, which is the same colour but about half the size. They also search the trees for grubs, etc. under the bark and in dead wood. The only woodpecker that does any damage, and this is in the summer, is the sapsucker. They make rows of holes in the trees, then come back and lick up the sap and insects attracted to it. To prevent further damage, spray or paint the affected area on the tree with pine tar just as though it were a pruning scar. The sapsuckers don't winter here.

You can have many hours of pleasure watching the chickadees and woodpeckers particularly if your feeder is close to your window. Also, if your feeder is by a window you can scare away the English sparrows when they come. They are most unwelcome around here because they steal the nests and chase away the good birds such as bluebirds and tree swallows. To discourage these sparrows from nesting, cover the holes on your nest boxes until the bluebirds return.

There are many other winter birds to be seen if you are always aware of a strange sound or shape. Occasionally both kinds of nuthatches, the White Breasted and the Red Breasted will come. They run down the tree trunks upside down peering in every nook and cranny for eggs and hibernating larvae. I have never had one at the feeder, but I know people in the district who have.

Hummingbird

Sometimes a big flock of Evening Grosbeaks will come. They love sunflower seeds and at today's prices they can cost a lot to feed. They are wanderers and will disappear as quickly as they came. One of their favourite foods are seeds of the Manitoba maple and the green ash.

I have occasionally had a small flock of White Winged Crossbills eating the seeds out of the spruce cones. The grosbeaks and crossbills probably don't do a great deal to benefit the garden, but it is so nice to see such colourful birds on a cold winter day. The males of the crossbills are a beautiful pink color and the Evening Grosbeaks have quite a bit of bright yellow on them.

The Bohemian Waxwings travel in flocks in the winter time. The mountain ash berries are their favourite food. They also like the fruit from the hawthorn, saskatoon, honeysuckle and cotoneaster. They occasionally eat the highbush cranberries. Those berries must be a bit too acid for the birds to make a feast on. I've seen the chickadees take one berry and eat some of it. Some of the highbush cranberries hang on for most of the winter without the birds bothering them.

We have another waxwing in the summer, the Cedar Waxwing. They are smaller and slimmer with a bit longer tail. The two birds are much the same with slight differences in their markings. Both birds have that lovely smooth look to them. They have a top knot and a black mask over their eyes.

The redpolls travel in large flocks in the winter and descend en masse on any patch of weeds or grass. They especially love the seeds of the pigweed. Quite often large flocks of snowbirds are seen. They also eat grass and weed seeds. Tree sparrows are another winter bird that travels in flocks eating seeds. They are one of the few birds that sing in the winter. They have a lovely canary-like song and to hear a flock of them singing on a cold winter day is something to remember.

The chickadees have a spring song, to me it always sounds like "spring's here" but I have heard them sing it in the dead of winter. It's very different from their familiar "see-dee-dee" call.

Chickadee

Our summer birds are too numerous to mention. In general, they are tremendous insect eaters. Even the many different kinds of sparrows which are seed eaters, feed their young on insects. I have seen eleven different kinds of sparrows in my yard in the spring. At this time I put the mixed wild bird seed in the feeder, and as well as eating at the feeder, they are constantly eating on the ground. This is especially true when we get our

April and May snow storms. There are hardly any chickweed plants in the garden and I'm sure it must be because of these beneficial seed eaters. Some of the little sparrows nest in the trees in the yard. I have found that as my spruce, pine and other trees and shrubs get larger, the bird population increases each year.

Regarding late snow storms which are peculiar to the foothills, birds migrate by the calendar, not by the weather, thus they can be devastated by these storms. To help them out, clear the snow from an area for birds such as robins which feed on grubs and worms and will not eat from feeders.

The robin truly is the harbinger of spring. Always digging for worms in the lawn and garden, robins make our spring evenings that much more pleasant by their cheerful songs.

In the spring there are many kinds of birds migrating. The warblers are beautiful little creatures. You

Robin

need a good pair of binoculars, lots of patience and an ear for any strange songs to identify them. They nearly always stay around the yard for a day or two. If you keep watching, quite often you are rewarded with a good look and then you can identify the bird. That is the advantage of knowing the different calls. If you hear something strange you know it is a new bird for your list. Quite a few of the warblers go on through and nest further north but some do stay around the Millarville district. Perhaps the best known one is the little yellow warbler. Some people call them the wild canary. I have heard the goldfinch called a canary as well. The goldfinch has the black wings, tail, and a spot on top of the head. The rest is bright yellow. They belong to the finch family, the same one that the sparrows belong to.

We have five different varieties of swallows and all of them practically live on mosquitoes. The cliff swallows, the ones that build the gourd-shaped mud nests, are discouraged from nesting on the house here, because a whole colony will move in. I just knock the nests down as soon as they start to build. That gives them lots of time to go to the barns and build under the eaves over there. The barn swallows also have a rust-coloured breast and a long forked tail. They aren't as social as the cliff swallows - just one pair nests by themselves. So I always let them build

144

their cup-shaped mud house where they want. I love to watch them dipping and diving around the house and through the trees catching insects on the wing. Then we have the little tree swallows nesting in the bird houses. They are the ones that nest in a lot of the bird houses along the roads. They have a dark blue back (it looks black) and a white breast.

Yellow Warbler

Getting back to the warblers, they have slim beaks and are strictly insect eaters. They generally nest in more wooded areas than they find around houses. During migration in the fall you see hundreds around the garden. At that time of year they are all rather drab in colour. The yellow rumped warbler is the one that we see so many of at this time of the year. They seem to be everywhere and for some reason you will see a mixed flock of bluebirds and warblers migrating together.

There are the different species of birds belonging to the flycatcher family that do their bit catching insects. The Kingbird, Phoebe, Wood Pewee and different species of flycatchers belong to this group. Sometimes they nest close to the buildings but they don't nest in bird houses.

We can't forget the saucy little House Wren who consumes a great many insects. They like a nest box with a hole about the size of a quarter. Nothing else can get into it then. I have a nest box quite close to one window and it's surprising how many insects those little birds bring while they are feeding the young. And the little male sings constantly while she is so busy. It's such a nice little bubbly song.

Of course one of our most beautiful summer birds is the Mountain Bluebird. They have been making a nice comeback the last few years after a disastrous snowstorm in June of 1951. The young were in the nests and the old birds got so cold and wet that they were dying, so naturally the young ones died too. For years after that you were lucky if you even saw one bluebird in a summer. Many people blame D.D.T. and the starlings; but it wasn't those, it was the snowstorm. They were completely wiped out in this district in two or three days. The bluebirds eat a great many cutworms. People are more aware of the birds now and they put up nest boxes which have helped the bluebirds make a comeback. I always have a family of bluebirds in a nest box. If the hole is no larger than 1½" across the starlings can't get in. As I am quick to discourage any English Sparrows I don't have any problem with them killing the young bluebirds and stealing the next boxes.

When I started watching birds you didn't tell people you were a birdwatcher for they thought you were a bit queer. Now many people do it. You will never be sorry if you encourage all the different birds to come around. Cats are the birds' worst enemy although some cats are worse than others. I have barn cats which you almost have to have to catch the mice, but these ones don't seem to bother the birds much. Of course I feed them which helps.

How to Attract the Birds

The more trees and shrubs, the more birds. Plant any kind of tree or shrub which produces fruit, berries, hips, haws, seeds or cones, such as: mountain ash, cotoneaster, choke-cherry, fruiting crabapples (see the Alberta Horticulture Guide), saskatoon, currants, highbush cranberry, Amur cherry, Nanking cherry, honeysuckle, Canada Buffaloberry, mayday, hawthorn, dogwood, all roses, Manitoba maple, green ash, junipers, spruce and pine. As well, plant sunflowers leaving the plants in the fall for the birds to eat the seeds.

Evergreens not only provide food, but winter shelter and year round refuge from predators. For this reason an ideal location for a bird bath or a feeder is near an evergreen tree.

Water is essential if you are attempting to attract birds. Put water in pans or basins if you are going to put up bird houses. It's best to elevate bird baths so the birds can see their enemies. A ten inch or twelve inch old disc off an old farm implement makes a good stand. This can be welded to a six or seven foot piece of pipe or it can be fitted on top of a post. You then place a pan or basin on top of the disc with some rocks in it so the birds have something to stand on as the water level goes down in the basin. Always place a piece of wood in your rain barrels and water troughs as birds have often drowned in these containers.

To discourage cats from climbing up poles or trees which hold nest boxes, wrap a 12 inch width of tin around the base of the trees or poles at a height of about six feet.

Upon adding a flock of bantam chickens to eat the slugs, one of our members discovered an increase in types and numbers of wild birds in this garden.

For those people who suffer from allergic reactions to wasp stings, it is worth noting that guinea fowl will eat great quantities of wasps.

What to Feed Birds

Place oatmeal, peanuts, sunflower seeds and commercial seed mix for wild birds in your feeders.

Hang fat in an onion bag from a branch.

Mix a bit of vegetable oil with equal parts of smooth peanut butter, ground suet and cracked wheat and spread over a ten inch long log which can be suspended from a branch. You may drill half inch holes in the log in which to put food although the natural indentations in the bark will hold the mixture nicely. It's a good idea to drill small holes in the log and insert sticks for the birds to perch on while they eat.

Place feeders under some sort of cover, such as two inch chicken wire, to keep the magpies away.

Fill a half empty coconut shell with left-over fat drippings in which you have mixed in rolled oats from the feed store.

Hang up a half a coconut with the white meat still in it, with strings. Using a darning needle you can thread peanuts in the shell on the strings.

Moistened dog kibble is a less expensive food which birds enjoy.

Bird House Construction
by Alex Lyall

Wood is the best material to use for the construction of bird houses. Softwoods such as cedar and white pine are the best. Hardwoods are rather difficult to drive nails into. You should use half-inch or three-quarter inch lumber.

There are several species of birds which will nest in bird houses. Some variations in the size of nest boxes are required for different birds.

Houses for bluebirds:
Dimensions:
5" x 6" inside
8" deep from peak of roof
6" from bottom of floor
1½" entrance hole

Houses for wrens and other small birds:
Dimensions:
4" x 4" inside
6" deep from peak of roof
4" from bottom of floor
1" entrance hole

A swing-out bottom can be fitted with a nail on each side and a screw nail in front. When the screw nail is removed the bottom will swing down for cleaning. Use non-rusting nails and screws.

BLUEBIRD HOUSE

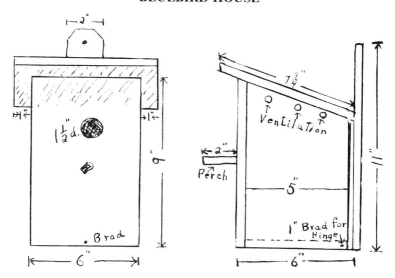

Dimensions and Location
   Floor of cavity - 5" x 6"
   Depth of cavity - 8"
   Entrance above floor - 6"
   Diameter of entrance - 1½"

Height above ground - 5' - 10'
In Open; Sunlit; - Some trees or posts

Left-over shingles are good to use for roofing. Put some sticky caulking compound under the shingle and nail down. This will keep the shingles from blowing off.

Bird houses should be ventilated. Drill some quarter inch holes up on the sides near the roof and on the ends.

Extend the roof on the front one inch and a half inches over the entrance hole. The rough side of the lumber should be put inside the house for the birds.

 **Helpful Hints**

To attract birds, cover pine cones with hardened bacon grease or other type of fat. Roll in bird seed and hang from a tree branch or tuck into bushes.

148

Grow currants next to raspberries. The birds prefer currants and will leave your raspberries alone.

Chapter Fifteen

The Country Garden

by *Dr. Mary J. Dover, O.B.E., C.M., L.L.D.*

The other day I unearthed a book of newspaper drawings "Barron's Calgary Cartoons", Vol. 1, 106 cartoons from the Albertan, price $1.00. No date but probably 1966. Across the top of most of the drawings an aeroplane is to be seen pulling an advertising banner bearing the legend "aren't the mountains pretty today?" A lovely idea - perhaps we all like yielding to its enchantment.

So we move into the country building on acreages of assorted sizes. Some buy a couple of horses, a dog and perhaps a cat and then all of a sudden it's spring - what about a garden?

Mine began with leveling the piles of earth thrown up from the basement and after a short discomfort with mud, the quick laying of sod.

Since then nearly 22 years have passed, there has been a great deal of planting. In the ditches beside the highways I found spruce and pine which I dug up and replanted. Today they are fine trees. Junipers found in pots at various garden centres and planted either beyond a stretch of lawn, outside a window, or within the plans where there has been clearing now are large, graceful, and of joy to waxwings and grosbeaks.

Fruit trees, shrubs and herbaceous plants have followed as well as clearing to make space for others. But over the years I must confess to study and learning and a quest for greater knowledge about the treasures of the earth and riches of the soil. The legacy which I found is a hilly spot, rich in native grass and wild flowers. There are woods, deep in their growth where throughout time animals have had the same pathways and where now I have the privilege of wandering.

After all the excitement of purchase, building and lawn right around

On Facing Page
A delightful blend of wild and cultivated flowers and shrubs.

the house there follows a surprising question. Where do we go from here? We buy books and magazines, join horticulture clubs, go to shows and end up wondering what it is all about. The biggest thing which comes our way is a huge mass of advice all free and often embarrassing or perhaps I mean conflicting.

I have come to a few conclusions over the years so for what they are worth I shall write down a short list.

The first is "Aren't the mountains pretty today." Here is the year round inspiration by which I live and also to show off to my visitors. Some of it is the view window.

One of my books has been a great interest and assistance. In "The Creative Art of Garden Design", published by Country Life, Percy Graves architect and landscape gardener, writes of glades. There are garden glades, woodland glades, also including borders, shrub selections for continuity of interest - all of which can be made into vistas. There is one lovely sentence. "There is a distinct difference between grandeur and beauty and just as grandeur comes of wide spaces and long distance and height in proportion, beauty belongs to more sophisticated scenes and can be created in smaller spaces."

My second conclusion arises from the wonderful fertility of the soil. The bunch grass, deep rooted and forever growing fed the buffalo throughout the hills from time immemorial and if cut early makes a splendid lawn. There are wild flowers of such abundance and colour that they never cease to make one marvel. Early explorers usually had botanists along in the expeditions. Hector was with Palliser, 1857-1860, and before that David Douglas (who found and named the fir which bears his name) sent an astonishing number and variety of seeds home which were successfully introduced into the gardens of Scotland and Britain. Douglas went just to what is now Oregon and Washington returning to Edinburgh going up the Columbia to Jasper and thence to York Factory in 1827. For the gardener here what a thrill. The Douglas fir prospers, so does the birch. Often unknowing we buy many of these plants.

There are other names - Centennial Crab, Hopa, Rudolph, Aurora, Spectabilis and Strathmore - all coloured, and the lovely whites Rescue and Dolgo and the pink budded "Johny Appleseed." This last is not the true name - it is the wild fruit which Johnny carried on his back handing the seeds to early settlers. One tree here is so beautiful. I searched for more finding them in Dauphin - I wanted them to grow along a new path so there are John, William, Tony, Andrew, Neil, Matthew and Gordon all to be seen from the windows.

Near the kitchen are two spruce. On their wedding eve Connie and her handsome John planted a blue, so a green joined it later.

The peony row came from Brooks but there have been additions by the careful green thumbs of Bob and Stanley who delighted in weeding them.

All the above names and plantings are illustrative of the fun gardening can be. It is another conclusion - that gardening is a year round occupation especially to occupy mind and time during the frosty months heading to the winter solstice and through the lengthening days when birds call their sounds and scillas and daffodils force up their green spears.

Somehow there is a conclusion with which I am unable to cope. I should like to have a collection of our wild roses. They are tall, medium and dwarf - crimson, pink, striped and white. They grow in unbelievable profusion and fill June and July with the delicate scent of summer. The silly thing is that having them all about me I have left them in their natural state and not brought them together.

All of this it is hoped will show that Oksi Hill is not a garden of an expert. It is a place of peace and frustration, of hope and wonderful thankfulness. Someday it may have finish of the first steps - but that is probably one hundred years hence.

 **Helpful Hints**

Spinach can be sown in August as the small plants will live over winter and you will have greens in May.

Peas can be sown in fall, they will come up in spring before the garden is ready to work. Cold nights don't hurt seedlings.

When onion seedlings you start inside reach 6" in height cut back to 3". When transplanting to garden trim both roots and tops.

Chapter Sixteen

The Millarville Horticultural Club's Ongoing Project

by Jon Lowry

The landscaping of the grounds of the historic log church at Millarville can serve to inspire other communities looking to beautify a local site. Begun in 1975, the project has succeeded due to well-organized volunteers working under the guidance of a master plan and drawing upon the horticultural expertise within the community.

In the early stages, before any planting was done, a five member Landscaping Committee was formed with the purpose of outlining all the things which a good landscape might do to improve the site. In this case, some areas of the site required shelter, other areas required ornamental plantings and still other spots, such as a proposed picnic area, required a combination of both. The committee also pinpointed several areas of the site with mature plantings which were difficult to maintain and as a result had become tangled and overgrown.

From the resulting list of problems and planting possibilities a rough master plan was drawn up and several copies blueprinted. The plan

---

On Facing Page

(1) Mulching the shrub borders; shrubs tied, soil surface contoured to form wells before poly is laid.

(2) Ornamental herculite gravel hides poly.

(3) Permanent mowing edge of treated 2 x 6 prevents lawn from creeping and holds gravel in place. All species are labelled through A.H.A. grant.

(4) Before project begins.

(5) After landscaping, native grouping graces sign; white spruce kept low and bushy, red osier dogwood and double wild rose in mulched bed.

(6) Potted ground covers will spread over gravel. Poplar planted through grant from Alberta 75th Birthday Celebration Fund.

(7) and (8) Octagonal planter anchors bare corner of hall and makes long building look wider. Double walled construction insulates roots for planting of Rocky Mountain juniper, Young's dwarf weeping birch and bergenia. Horticultural Club maintains annuals in pockets not mulched with plastic and gravel.

drawing which is still in use allows the Landscaping Committee to decide priorities and stage the work over a number of years. Each stage is then broken down into a number of tasks which can be carried out in two or three work bees every season.

To initiate a particular stage of the project the committee meets early in the year. Optional solutions are discussed and detailed drawings are prepared from which to estimate the amount and cost of materials and the possible hours of labour involved.

In designing a particular stage of the project such as walkways or planters there are two elements which set some limits on the plans. On the one hand, it has been found that whatever is built has to match the skills and abilities of the volunteers and should not require having to engage professional contractors. Also, to keep expenses at a minimum it is important to determine what materials might be donated or purchased at a discount and to plan accordingly. For example, where landscaping of the church hall called for construction of a rather complicated eight-sided planter, it was found that a local contractor was willing to donate his expertise in overseeing a work crew of home handymen. Had this not occurred, an alternate plan did allow for a more simple rectangular planter. On another occasion, gravel which had to come from a great distance was needed to resurface and clearly define a proper parking area. One alternative called for gravelling only a small area until it was learned that a local trucker was willing to do the hauling free of charge.

Though all labour for this project has been of a volunteer nature and a great proportion of the materials donated, there is always a point where money must be spent and funds collected to pay the bills. In this case, because a number of clubs and organizations including the Horticultural Club use the church hall as a regular meeting place, several groups have generously contributed to the financing of this project. Also, where some aspects of the project, such as labelling the plant material or applying poly and mulch, have an educational purpose, funding in the form of grants has come through the Alberta Horticultural Association.

In applying for grants or seeking private donations, it has been found that the existence of a master plan and a set of easily understood drawings, together with the proof of results from the earliest stages, all serve to provide a good impression of a well-organized project. This impression greatly helps to attract outside assistance. Most grants are offered on a matching basis. Whenever the Club treasury is unable to supply all the cash for its own portion of expenses, a monetary value is assigned to the amount of donated labour, estimated on how many hours a given stage of the project will take to complete.

The business of ongoing garden maintenance has provided some valuable lessons and demonstrated the need for flexibility in scheduling the various stages. For example, in 1976 the first major work bee was held to do planting of a 1200 foot long tree and shrub border on the northeast side of the site. Organizers were overwhelmed when about 60 energetic volunteers turned up and completed planting in a matter of hours. However, when it later came time to weed, water and maintain this extensive planting, the task fell on the shoulders of an overworked few. It involved hauling tools and rototillers to the site and filling drums of water at a nearby riverford to bale onto the plants. All this was in addition to the regular (or at times irregular) mowing of about 5 acres of prairie wool.

Ultimately this original planting did survive and thrive. Nevertheless, though the master plan called for more planting in each of the following years, much of it was delayed until the problems of maintenance were finally settled. Several steps have been taken. On the one hand, instead of more new planting, it was decided to go back to the long tree and shrub border and set things straight. This area was carefully cleaned of weeds using systemic herbicides, then completely framed with a mowing edge of treated 2x6 planks. In later steps and with financial assistance from the AHA, the need for cultivating or extensive watering has been eliminated through the innovation of mulching with 6 mil poly and ornamental gravel. As a result, the dozens of plants there are now thriving beyond our greatest expectations. A similar treatment of framing and mulching is being applied to all other new plantings and around some of the older trees and shrubs which predate this project. Maintenance of all such areas is now simply a question of pruning and fertilizing once or twice a year; chores which can be handled by a handful of volunteers in less than two hours.

More recently, the task of watering or applying water-soluble fertilizers has been eased thanks to the installation of an underground water line and a number of taps. Many of the tools and other paraphernalia necessary to good yard management are now stored on the site (although a garden shed installed in the willows blew away during a blast of chinook wind a couple of years ago). Also, to better cope with lawn maintenance and minor grooming chores, a number of individual work crews have been organized drawing from members of the Church, the Horticultural Club and the community at large. Each crew takes on a two week stint between May and September. There always seems to be someone who doesn't mind a lot of phoning to set up the crews and sort out their schedules. Each crew has a leader whose job it is to allocate the tasks according to his helpers' likes and capabilities. Meanwhile, the Horticultural Club specifically tends to the growing and care of annuals around the Church hall and dressing up the grounds for the annual Flower Festival sponsored by the Women's Guild each August.

Altogether then, it appears that a long-term project will keep its momentum if it incorporates: **A) A fair and even distribution of the work**

load and a division of labour. When busy folk have their own gardens to tend, no one is anxious to devote unlimited time to a community garden where there is no clear cut beginning or end. On the other hand, by dividing the project into bite-size stages, having different groups tend to different areas of concern and generally seeing to it that no one person is expected to contribute more than 8 or 10 hours a year, helpers are more apt to turn up willingly. **B) Every possible means of minimizing manual labour.** Many of the tricks and innovations used in this project have shown volunteers how to actually minimize some of the drudgery in their own gardens.

Hence, planning for maintenance should be an integral part of any community beautification plan that involves planting. If it will be difficult to find enough hands to take care of weeding and watering on a large scale, the plantings should be kept minimal and done in stages phased over a number of seasons. The secret to success in the chinook zone is to get the plants well-established with tender loving care in the first one or two seasons after planting. Community volunteers will not lose their enthusiasm if ten trees are planted every year for five years and well cared for rather than planting 50 trees at one time and losing half of them.

The Church site is located on Secondary highway 549 between Okotoks and Highway 22. Visitors are always welcome.

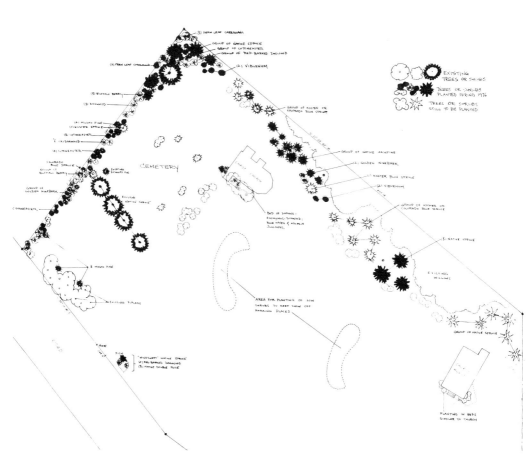

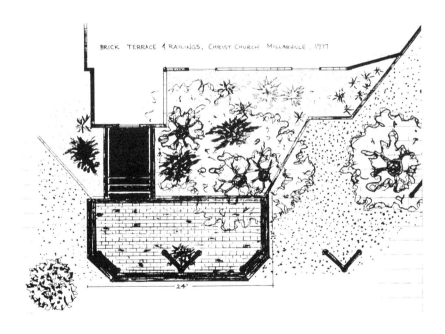

BRICK TERRACE & RAILINGS, CHRIST CHURCH MILLARVILLE, 1977

24'

Chapter Seventeen

Recipes for Garden Produce

Soups

CREAM OF CAULIFLOWER SOUP

1 cauliflower
4 cups milk
1½ cups vegetable stock or water
4 tablespoons butter

4 tablespoons plain flour
salt and pepper
chopped parsley

Cut cauliflower into flowerets and rinse in cold water. Combine the milk and stock or water and bring to boil. Add cauliflower and cook until tender. Press with liquid through strainer or puree in electric blender. In large saucepan, melt butter and stir in flour. Cook for 2 minutes over low heat. Slowly pour into cauliflower mixture, stirring constantly, until smooth. Add salt and pepper to taste and cook for 10 minutes. Serve sprinkled with chopped parsley.

CREAM OF TOMATO SOUP

First, cut up and blend skins and all, as many tomatoes as you have on hand to use up. Measure the quantity, then put on to heat slowly. Meanwhile, make an equal quantity of white sauce. Toss into tomato juice, a few bits of celery leaves and some green onions, some chopped parsley and anything else found still growing in the herb patch. Add salt and pepper to taste. When sauce has thickened, let both mixtures cool to the same temperature, then slowly pour the red into the white, stirring gently. This will prevent curdling. You may also add a sprinkling of brown sugar and dash of soya sauce and good dollop of parmesan cheese. Even soup haters will ask for more of this one.

FRENCH POTATO SOUP
(Potage Parmentier)

6 medium potatoes
2 large carrots
2 onions
4 sticks celery

Thyme, pepper, salt, parsley to taste
1 gal. beef stock or water and beef
    soup base
5-6 slices bacon

Peel potatoes and clean vegetables. Cut in fairly large pieces. Saute them all first in ½ cup oil for 2-3 minutes. Add the stock, thyme and pepper. Cook for about one hour. Sieve or put through the blender. Return to cooking pot. Cut bacon in small pieces and fry until crisp. Add fat and bacon to soup. Add the finely chopped parsley. Serve with croutons. Serves 9-10.

HINT - Use other vegetables, such as broccoli, cabbage, green beans, corn, zucchini added to above. Make a big batch and freeze in cartons. Use ham, sausage or wieners in place of bacon.

MINESTRONE

1 small head of celery
1 small zucchini - sliced
2 large carrots - diced very thin
½ small cabbage - shredded
½ lb. skinned tomatoes
2 leeks - sliced
4 pints stock or water (if water used, add ½ cup chicken soup base)
4 oz. salt pork or streaky bacon - diced
4 oz. spaghetti cooked separately, chopped - do not overcook
8 oz. diced potatoes (optional)
1 small can tomato paste
¼ cup finely chopped parsley
salt, pepper, oregano, thyme, a bayleaf, marjoram to taste
4 oz. Parmesan cheese
1 onion - sliced
1 garlic - crushed

Fry the bacon in a little oil, (do not brown) then add onions, carrots and other vegetables except the parsley and zucchini. Saute for 2-3 minutes. Add to boiling stock. Simmer for about 50 minutes. Add the zucchini, parsley and spaghetti, season to taste. Stir Parmesan cheese into the soup before serving. Leftover soup may be frozen. It reconstitutes very well. Other vegetables may be added as well.

Salads

BEET MOLD

2½ tablespoons gelatin
½ cup cold water
1 lb. diced cooked beets
¼ cup vinegar
¼ cup lemon juice
⅔ cup sugar
1 teaspoon salt

¼ teaspoon black pepper
1 cup chopped celery
1 cup chopped cucumber
2 scallions - chopped
shredded cabbage
sour cream

Soak the gelatin in cold water for 5 minutes. Mix together the beets, lemon juice, sugar, salt and pepper. Press through a sieve or puree in electric blender. Pour the beet mixture into a saucepan and heat to boiling. Stir in the gelatin until dissolved. Cool, then chill until partially set. Add chopped celery, cucumber and scallions. Mix thoroughly. Pour into an oiled mold and chill until set. Unmold onto a bed of shredded cabbage and garnish with sour cream.

CABBAGE SALAD

1 large cabbage shredded finely
2 large onions shredded finely or sliced finely
1 teaspoon salt mixed with ¾ cup sugar

In large bowl, put vegetables in layers with sugar and salt and cover (I use gallon-size ice cream pails). Mix ¼ cup sugar with 2 teaspoons dry mustard and add to 1 cup vinegar (white). Bring to boil. Add ¾ cup salad oil to hot vinegar mixture, cool slightly and pour over vegetables. Put either 3 teaspoons celery seed or a mixture of pickling spices in cloth bag and push down into salad. Cover and keep in fridge. Will keep for a month.

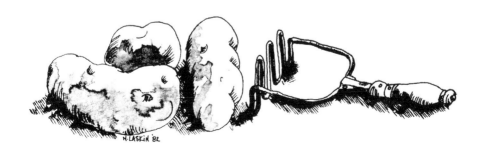

CAULIFLOWER AND CARROT SALAD

¾ lb. cauliflower
4 medium carrots
1 medium onion - chopped
1 teaspoon sugar

⅔ cup mayonnaise
2½ tablespoons lemon juice
salt and pepper
lettuce leaves

Chop the cauliflower into small pieces. Grate carrots and mix with cauliflower and onion. Blend together the sugar, mayonnaise, lemon juice, salt and pepper to taste. Pour over the cauliflower mixture and toss thoroughly. Serve on crisp lettuce leaves.

COLE SLAW

2 heads cabbage - shredded fine
6 carrots - shredded fine
2 onions - chopped fine

2 red peppers - sweet
½ cup salt

Cover with cold water. Let sit 3 hours. Drain well. Pack into jars, leave ½ inch headspace.

Boil together:
    1 quart white vinegar
    5 cups sugar
Pour into jars. Seal.

1 teaspoon celery seed
1 teaspoon mustard seed

COMFREY SALAD

1 cup pea sprouts or fresh peas
1 cup chopped comfrey
¼ cup green onions

½ cup grated carrot
¼ cup chopped parsley or
    1 tablespoon dried

Dressing:
    ¼ cup oil
    ¼ cup lemon juice
    ¼ cup chopped fresh mint (1 tablespoon dried)
    kelp or spurolina

EVERLASTING SALAD

1 cabbage
5 carrots
4 onions
4 peppers
1 teaspoon celery seed

1 teaspoon mustard seed
¼ cup salt
2 cups sugar
2 cups vinegar (white)

Shred vegetables, add salt and let stand 2 hours. Drain well and add other ingredients. Put in jars and keep refrigerated. This salad can be processed in hot water bath for 20 minutes in sealed jars.

ZUCCHINI SALAD #1

2 lbs. zucchini	½ teaspoon salt
1 teaspoon salt	1½ oz. cream cheese - cubed
3 egg yolks	3 hard-boiled eggs - sliced
1 teaspoon dry mustard	½ cup wine vinegar
½ cup oil	lettuce

Wash, cut off ends, but do not pare zucchini. Slice thinly and sprinkle with salt. Let stand for ½ hour. Drain and put in bowl. Blend egg yolks, mustard and oil. Pour over, zucchini, sprinkle with salt and pepper. Serve on lettuce, garnish with cheese and hard-boiled eggs. Pour vinegar over all.

ZUCCHINI SALAD #2

1 lb. zucchini	½ cup chopped onion
2 cups water	½ cup chopped green pepper
½ teaspoon salt	½ cup celery
1 clove garlic	French dressing

Cut zucchini in bite size pieces. Cook in boiling, salted water for 3 minutes. Remove from heat, let stand 2 minutes. Drain and chill. Rub cut garlic clove over inside of salad bowl. Place ingredients in bowl, toss with dressing. Makes 6 servings.

KIDNEY BEAN ZUCCHINI SALAD

3 tablespoons salad oil	3 tablespoons white vinegar
3 medium zucchini - thinly sliced	2 teaspoons sugar
2 medium onions - sliced	2 teaspoons salt
1 large green pepper - cut into 1'' pieces	¼ teaspoon pepper
1 vegetable bouillon cube or envelope	
1 - 15 oz. can red kidney beans - drained	

Early in the day or the day before serving: In skillet, over medium high heat, in hot salad oil, cook zucchini, onions, green pepper and bouillon cube until vegetables are tender, crisp, and bouillon cube is dissolved, about 5 minutes. Remove from heat, stir in kidney beans, vinegar, sugar, salt and pepper. Spoon mixture into large bowl, cover and refrigerate until well chilled. Makes 8 servings.

Vegetables

ASPARAGUS - ALMOND BUTTER SAUCE

Cook ¼ cup slivered almonds in ¼ cup butter over low heat till golden brown, about 5-7 minutes, stirring constantly. Remove from heat, add ½ teaspoon salt, 1 tablespoon lemon juice and pour over cooked asparagus.

Bacon Bits: fry 2-3 slices bacon till crisp, crumple and add to cooked asparagus.

CREAMY GREEN BEANS

Soften one 3 oz. package cream cheese. Blend in 1 tablespoon milk, ¼ teaspoon celery seed, ¼ teaspoon salt. Add to cooked green beans and heat through. Or substitute ½ teaspoon dill weed for the celery seed.

ELEGANT GREEN BEANS

4 cups green beans	2 tablespoons vinegar
¼ cup chopped onion	¼ cup snipped parsley
3 tablespoons butter or margarine	1 cup dairy sour cream
2 tablespoons all-purpose flour	3 slices bacon - cooked crisp
2 tablespoons sugar	

Drain beans, saving 1 cup liquid. Saute onion in butter till soft. Stir in flour. Stir in bean liquid, sugar, vinegar and parsley. Cook stirring constantly, till thickened. Add sour cream and pour over beans; heat through but do not boil. Crumble bacon over top. Makes 6-8 servings.

FROZEN GREEN BEANS

Boil beans one minute. Cool. Put in freezer bag, cover with water, add enough salt for cooking, tie bag securely and freeze package. To serve, turn out of freezer bag into pot and put on stove at medium heat. Soon ice will melt and when it comes to boil, remove and serve immediately. The taste and texture of the beans is excellent.

BROCCOLI SUPREME

1½ lbs. broccoli	½ cup sour cream
3 tablespoons butter	2 teaspoons prepared horseradish
2½ tablespoons flour	salt, pepper, ¼ teaspoon thyme.

Trim broccoli and cook in boiling salted water until tender. Drain and reserve ½ cup of the liquid. Melt butter in saucepan and stir in flour. Cook over low heat 1 minute. Slowly add reserved liquid, stirring constantly until thick and smooth. Add sour cream, horseradish, salt, pepper to taste and thyme. Put broccoli on serving dish and pour sauce over. Serve immediately.

CARROTS WITH HONEY

1 lb. carrots	2½ tablespoons honey
1 cup vegetable stock or water	4 teaspoons butter
salt	

Peel carrots if necessary and cut into slices. Bring vegetable stock or water to boil and add carrots. Cover and simmer until carrots are tender. Drain. Season to taste with salt. Stir in honey and butter until both are melted and carrots are thoroughly coated.

LEEKS AU GRATIN

2 lb. leeks	1 cup milk
3 tablespoons butter	salt
4 tablespoons flour	nutmeg
½ cup vegetable stock or water	⅔ cup grated cheese

Trim roots and damaged outer leaves. Quarter leeks and wash thoroughly in running water. Place in saucepan with about ½ cup of water, cover, cook over medium heat until tender. Drain if necessary. Keep warm. Melt butter in saucepan, stir in flour. Cook over low heat for 1 minute. Slowly add vegetable stock or water, stirring constantly, until smooth. Blend in milk, continuing to stir until smooth and thick. Add salt and nutmeg to taste and half the cheese. Stir until cheese is melted. Butter baking dish and place leeks in it. Pour cheese sauce over leeks and sprinkle remaining cheese on top. Bake in 350⁰F oven for ½ hour. Serve immediately.

MASHED PARSNIPS

1 lb. parsnips   1 medium onion - chopped
½ lb. potatoes   3 tablespoons butter
salt   chopped parsley

Trim and peel parsnips and cut into thick slices. Cook in boiling, salted water until tender. Peel potatoes and cut into chunks. Cook in boiling, salted water until tender. Mash parsnips and potatoes separately, then mix together. Add salt to taste and half the butter, beat until smooth. Saute onion in remaining butter until golden brown. Put parsnip mixture on serving dish and pour on the onion and butter. Sprinkle with chopped parsley and serve immediately.

PIGWEED OR LAMBS QUARTERS

Boil young pigweed until tender, then put in cold water and strain. Run through food chopper with some onion tops or whole onion. Cook in hot butter with salt and nutmeg. Garnish with hard boiled egg.

SCALLOPED POTATOES AND CARROTS

2 tablespoons butter   2 tablespoons flour
1 teaspoon salt   ⅛ teaspoon pepper
2 cups milk

Melt butter, blend in flour and seasonings. Gradually add milk and cook until smooth and thick. To mixture, add 4 cups thinly sliced potatoes, 1 cup sliced carrots, 1 cup sliced onions, and bring to boil. Turn into greased baking dish. Cover and bake 30 minutes at 350°F. Remove cover and continue baking until potatoes are tender (about 25 minutes more).

SPEEDY SCALLOPED POTATOES

2 potatoes - peeled and sliced thin
1 onion - peeled and sliced thin
1 cup milk
1 tablespoon butter
salt and pepper

Put potatoes and onion in frying pan with ½ cup water, a little salt and cook until barely tender, about 6-7 minutes. Add 1 cup milk, 1 table-spoon butter, 2 tablespoons grated cheese or Cheese Whiz, pepper to taste. Thicken with a little flour and milk. This is a quick and tasty way to cook potatoes if in a hurry or unexpected company drops in. Serves 2-3.

FROZEN TOMATOES

Scald, peel, stew with salt and sugar to taste and place in freezer bag or other container and freeze.

FROZEN TOMATO PUREE

A quick, easy and effective way to preserve tomatoes when they all come ripe at once. Just cut up some tomatoes that have a blemish or are over-ripe but still usable, put in blender, whiz them up, skins and all, pour into plastic picnic cups and freeze. When frozen you can easily pop them out of their cups and put them all in one big plastic bag in the deep freeze. Next time you have a recipe which calls for one cup tomato puree, just get one measured frozen lump from bag and hey presto. No vitamins are lost by cooking in this method. Great in stews or Italian type dishes.

TOMATOES VERTIS

8 large tomatoes	4 tablespoons butter
2 medium carrots	1 egg - beaten
1 medium green pepper	1 cup dried bread crumbs
1 medium onion	½ cup milk
2 stalks celery	½ teaspoon salt
2 cups chopped spinach	¼ teaspoon black pepper
1½ tablespoon parsley	grated cheese

Cut thin slice from top of tomatoes. Scoop out pulp. Chop all the vegetables coarsely and put through mincer. Melt butter, add vegetables and simmer until brown. Add egg, bread crumbs, milk, salt and pepper. Mix well, then fill the tomatoes. Sprinkle with grated cheese and put in buttered baking dish. Bake in 400°F oven for about 20 minutes or until tomatoes are tender.

TURNIP WHIP

3 teaspoons instant chicken bouillon granules	1 tablespoon butter or margarine
2 lbs. turnips (about 7 cups)	1 tablespoon parsley
2 tablespoons chopped onion	½ teaspoon sugar

In large saucepan, combine bouillon and 3 cups water. Heat until granules dissolve and water is boiling. Add turnips (which have been peeled and cubed) and simmer until tender. Drain. In same saucepan, cook onion in butter. With electric mixer, whip turnips until fluffy. Mixture will not be smooth. Stir parsley, onion and sugar into turnips.

VEGETABLE CURRY

1 lb. green beans - cut into pieces	1 cup fresh peas
2 medium potatoes - peeled and diced	2 teaspoons mustard seed
	2 teaspoons tumeric
½ lb. carrots - sliced	1 teaspoon ground coriander
⅓ cup butter	½ teaspoon cayenne
2 teaspoons cumin seeds	2½ tablespoons lemon juice
1½ teaspoons salt	1 cup yogurt

Mix together - green beans, potatoes and carrots and put into saucepan with enough water to just cover. Bring to boil. Reduce heat, cover and cook for 5 minutes. Remove from heat but do not drain. Heat butter in large saucepan. Add spices and gently cook for 2 minutes. Add vegetables with their liquid and the lemon juice. Mix well. Bring to boil, then add yogurt and peas. Reduce heat and cook over gentle heat for 30 minutes.

ZUCCHINI

When choosing zucchini, try to pick small, young specimens that are firm. They can be baked, boiled, steamed, stuffed, scalloped; used in salads, main dishes, vegetables, quick breads, cakes etc. Your imagination is the limit with zucchini! Zucchini can also be frozen for later use in quick breads or casseroles.

STIR-FRIED VEGETABLES

Use any combination of fresh vegetables. Wash and prepare them all before you start. Slicing diagonally does not make them taste any different but is attractive. Use a variety of colors, textures and flavours such as onions, carrots, edible pea pods, celery, asparagus, green beans, broccoli or cauliflower, cabbage, etc. Start with a hot wok or heavy saucepan. Add ¼ cup oil. Begin with vegetables which take longest to cook. A little garlic and a thin slice of fresh ginger fried first and discarded, adds flavor to oil. Add vegetables one kind at a time, stirring all the time. Do not overcook. The secret of stir-fried vegetables is to serve them tender-crisp. When all vegetables are in, add ½ cup chicken stock, 2 tablespoons soya sauce, salt and pepper to taste. Sprinkle with toasted sesame seeds if desired. Sauce may be thickened slightly with cornstarch if desired. Serve immediately.

VEGETABLE SPAGHETTI

Vegetable spaghetti is a novelty squash that looks like a plate of spaghetti after it has been cooked. It is rather stringy and coarse in texture compared to other squash. When raw, this squash has a delicious, nutty flavor and can be used shredded or diced in salads.

Preparation:

Boiled - Cook the squash whole for about 30 minutes in boiling water. Cut in half. Scoop out the seeds. Pull the spaghetti-like pulp from the shell, and serve.

Baked - Cut in half and remove seeds. Bake in an uncovered pan at 350°F. If you wish, a few strips of bacon may be placed over the cut edges. This method takes about 1 hour. Or, use a little water in the pan, put the lid on and let the vegetables steam. The pulp should pull away from the shell and produce thin, spaghetti-like strands, ready to top with your favorite topping.

Toppings - Be creative and don't be afraid to experiment. Here are a few suggestions:

Serve vegetable spaghetti hot with -
Salt, pepper and butter
Canadian cheddar cheese sauce
Parmesan cheese, sprinkled on top
Tomato and meat sauce
In a casserole as a substitute for pasta
Serve cold with Mayonnaise or French Dressing.

EARLY SPRING GREENS

Pick dandelion plants before flowers appear. Wash thoroughly. Take equal portions of bacon fat and vinegar. Season with salt and pepper and pour over greens just before serving.

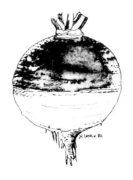

Special Section

SAUERKRAUT

Extra cabbage can easily be made into this old fashioned vegetable. If you feel like experimenting with a small batch, a gallon jar will hold slightly over 5 lbs. of cabbage or a 2 gallon crock holds 15 lbs. cabbage. Choose sound, mature cabbage, use 1 lb. salt for 40 lbs. of cabbage or 2 teaspoons salt for 1 lb. cabbage. European flavor can be added with use of dill, a bay leaf, few garlic cloves, peeled but whole so that they can be fished out before serving; or onion rings or some favorite whole pickling spice.

Never mix a fresh batch of sauerkraut with one already fermenting. A top quality vegetable should release enough juice to form a covering brine in about 24 hours. If it hasn't, bring level above shredded cabbage by adding a weak brine on the proportions of 1.5 teaspoons of pickling salt for each cup of cold water.

Method — Remove outside leaves, quarter heads and cut out cores. Slice cabbage fine into $\frac{1}{16}$ inch shreds and mix with pickling salt. Pack containers with alternate layers of salt and cabbage, as in amount indicated above. Tamp every 2 layers of cabbage to get rid of trapped air and start the juice flow. Tap gently with clean wooden potato masher or bottom of small jar or clean baseball bat. Pack firmly in jars or crocks to within 2 inches of top. Cover with clean cloth and a plate or any board except pine. Place weight on plate, heavy enough to make the brine come up to the cover and wet the cloth. When fermentation begins, remove scum daily and replace clean cloth over the cabbage. Wash plate daily also.

Best quality kraut results when made at a temperature below 60°F, requiring at least a month of fermentation. It may be cured in less time at higher temperature, but the kraut will not be as good. If sauerkraut turns tan, too much juice has been lost in the fermenting process. When fermenting ceases, store kraut in cool place, if it is not around 38°F you had better process it. For the canning process, heat kraut to simmering temperature (about 180°F), pack firmly into hot jars; add sufficient kraut juice or weak brine (2 tablespoons salt to 1 quart water) to cover, leaving ½ inch head space. Process in boiling water bath, 25 minutes, for pints 30 minutes. Cook kraut 15 minutes before serving.

SPROUTS
Dorothy Jackson

Imagine a vegetable that is ready to eat in 3-6 days; does not need soil or sunlight, can be grown by anyone, at home and indoors, needs little attention, grows well all year round and is outstandingly nutritious. The sprouting of seeds for food, may one day become a mainstay of our nutritional survival. Research shows that sprouts are among the highest in natural vitamin content per serving of any food obtainable, with many of the varieties of sprouts increasing tremendously in vitamin B and C during the sprouting process.

Seeds, grains, nuts and beans are alive in suspended animation awaiting the simple conditions needed to burst into full life, providing a harvest of fresh food every few days, in any season and climate at low cost. Sprouting is easy, fun, and the whole family can partake.

You Can Sprout:
Alfalfa - one of the most popular sprouts, delicious in sandwiches or in salads. Use when first green leaves appear. Wheat - resembles fresh corn just picked, for the starches in the wheat are degraded to the same sugars found in corn. It should be used when the sprout is the same length as seed, just ½ inch.

You can also sprout barley, rye, corn millet, oats, peas, chick peas, fenugreek seeds, lentils, soybeans, mung beans, mustard seeds, radish seeds, chia seeds, cabbage seeds, flax seeds, clover, peanuts, sunflower seeds, buckwheat, cress, sesame seeds, etc.

Just about any bean or seed can be sprouted, but potato and tomato sprouts are poisonous. Make sure seeds used are untreated with mould retardants, fungicides or insecticides.

The equipment needed for sprouting can be as simple as a jar with nylon net or cheesecloth fastened over the top with an elastic band. Plastic lids with various sized screens can be purchased for use on standard, wide mouth mason jars. For the more enthusiastic sprouter, various styles of trays are available. Only use a small amount of seed, 1-2 teaspoons, as they increase in volume by the time they are ready to eat. 1 tablespoon of dry alfalfa seeds provide 1 quart of sprouts.

The recipe is a cinch. You just add water and you rinse often. Wash the seeds thoroughly, soak overnight, drain and continue to rinse several times per day, using coolish or tepid water. Use average room temperature for growing (60°-75°F). If sprouting seeds smell slightly, freshen up with a clear water rinse or grow under cooler conditions.

Use sprouts as soon as they are ready and store any surplus in the refrigerator. Rinse if necessary, with cold water before serving. The soak and rinse water from most sprouts is full of valuable nutrients. You can use it for making soups, teas, or even watering your plants.

Ways to use Sprouts:

Soups - Add just before serving. Rye sprouts taste like wild rice.

Casseroles - Add just before serving.

Salads - Tossed, fruit, three bean, Waldorf; let the seed sprouts get their first primary leaves and toss with any salad.

Sandwiches - Use instead of lettuce.

Eggs - In omelets, souffles, scrambled eggs or:

Grind sprouts in meat grinder and add to final kneading of breads or stir into muffins, waffle and pancake batter.

Eat - Rye and wheat sprouts as a snack like peanuts

In sandwich spreads - as a crunchy replacement for celery

Stew - with tomatoes

Marinate - and serve raw

As a vegetable - steamed, sauteed or baked.

Most sprouts should never be cooked more than 5-8 minutes, or the taste, texture and nutritional value may be lost. Soy beans may need an extra 10 minutes of steaming. Let your imagination be your guide when using sprouts. Experiment, eat some sprouts every day. They contain vitamins, minerals, proteins and enzymes that multiply during sprouting and are a natural source of fibre. Sprouts are one of the few known complete foods. They are low in carbohydrates and calories, but rich in essential nutrients. When nuts are sprouted, the fat content is reduced.

Alfalfa Sprout Toss

2 cups finely chopped celery	1 cup currants
1 cup alfalfa sprouts	2 grated carrots

Mix ingredients thoroughly and chill until ready to serve. Serve on individual salad plates topped with yogurt dressing. Serves 4-6 people.

Alfalfa Omelet

6 egg whites - beaten stiff	½ teaspoon sea salt
6 egg yolks - lightly beaten	½ cup grated cheese
¼ cup milk or cream	1½ tablespoons butter
1 cup alfalfa sprouts	

Mix egg yolks, salt and cheese. Fold egg whites and sprouts into egg yolk mixture. Melt butter in large frying pan. Pour all of omelet mixture into pan. Cover and cook over low heat until firm. Fold omelet over and gently lift onto warm platter. Serves 4.

Sprout and Mushroom Salad

2 cups alfalfa sprouts
1 cup bean sprouts
1 cup sliced mushrooms

½ cup diced, cooked, potato
½ cup cooked peas

Combine ingredients. Chill. Toss with favorite dressing just before serving. 6 servings.

Sprouted Wheat Balls (Candy)

1 cup wheat sprouts
1 cup nuts

1 cup coconut
1 cup raisins

Grind and mix well. Shape into balls and roll in fine coconut or wheat germ. Keep refrigerated. 1 cup cream cheese can be used instead of coconut. Instead of raisins, any dried fruit can be used to give wheat balls a different flavor.

Wheat Sprout Stuffing

The sprouts are slightly chewy in the bread dressing and the taste is delicious.

1 small onion - chopped
2 stalks celery - chopped
1 cup wheat sprouts
1 cup whole wheat bread crumbs

2 tablespoons melted butter
1 teaspoon salt
½ teaspoon pepper, sage and
    thyme

Chop onions and celery until fine. Toss with sprouts and crumbs. Pour melted butter over all and toss again. Add salt, pepper, sage and thyme. Will stuff a 3-4 pound fowl.

Rye Sprout Pilaf

4 tablespoons butter
1 cup sprouted rye or wheat
    - drained well
½ cup water or consomme

½ lb. mushrooms - sliced
2 tablespoons chopped parsley
1 teaspoon salt

Melt butter in pan and saute sprouts and mushrooms 5 minutes. Add water or consomme, simmer until evaporated. Season with salt, garnish with parsley.

Breakfast Salad

2 cups wheat sprouts
1 cup sunflower seeds - hulled
3 apples with skins - grated

½ cup raisins
½ cup yogurt
3 bananas - sliced

Lightly toss all ingredients together in salad bowl. Refrigerate until ready to serve.

Crunchy Sprout Salad

Sprouts add a textural variation to molded gelatin salads and add a delightful taste as well.

1 package unflavored gelatin	½ cup shredded cabbage
4 tablespoons cold water	½ cup grated carrots
2 cups boiling water	½ cup chopped celery
juice and grated rind of 1 lemon	½ cup sprouted mung beans
1 teaspoon salt	½ cup sprouted wheat
2 tablespoons chopped chives	

Soak gelatin in cold water. Dissolve in boiling water. Add lemon juice, rind and salt. Chill. When partly set, add the vegetables and pour into mold.

SUGAR SNAP PEAS

The gardeners who like to grow regular "snow peas" for stir frying or steaming will be pleased with "Sugar Snap". Unlike flat podded sugar or snow peas which should be eaten when the pods are small, "Sugar Snap" remains in prime condition for days. Round pods with very thick walls can be eaten at fully mature sizes, 2½ to 3 inches in length.

Mature pods require stringing. This can be accomplished quickly and conveniently while you are snapping the pods into bite-size pieces. Should any pods over grow and start to yellow, you can shell them and combine the green peas with the edible pods. Snap peas can yield two to three times as much marketable food as shell peas or standard edible pods varieties. Edible podded peas are nutritious and filling but not as high in total carbohydrates and fats as green shelled peas. The crunchy pods contain fibre, vitamins and some carbohydrates.

If you cook "Sugar Snap" pods, don't overdo it; lightly steam or stir fry in oil to retain a hint of crispness. Over-cooking will make pods come apart and be too soft. If you are adding them to other vegetables, do so just 2 minutes before serving. "Sugar Snap" is easy to freeze but cannot be canned. The high temperature in canning destroys the structure of the pods.

Sugar Snap Omelet

Prepare your favorite omelet recipe. When it is almost cooked, arrange cooked Sugar Snaps in centre. Fold omelet over and serve it hot.

176

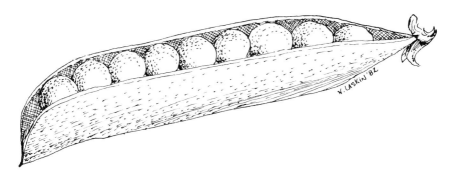

Sugar Snaps also makes great cocktail rolls. Make them a few hours ahead and store them, covered, in the refrigerator. Use squares of thinly sliced cheese, ham or other sandwich meats and roll the squares around strung, fresh Sugar Snaps. Skewer the rolls shut with toothpicks, garnish with olives, cocktail onions, radish slices, carrot curls, and anything else you can dream up that's colorful and tasty. Another idea for a cocktail plate is to shell the peas and leave pods attached at one end. Stuff with cheese mixture that has had some of the shelled peas that have been mashed, added to it. Circle the stuffed pods around a chunk of cheese and serve with a dish of crackers.

The next time you serve a vegetable dip, add some mashed, shelled peas to it and use the pods with ends left attached as a scoop for the dip. Dips or stuffings that contain mashed peas have better pea flavor if allowed to stand overnight in the fridge. Pods will remain crisp if stored in plastic bags in the fridge. Sugar Snaps can be added to almost any vegetable stir fry, casserole, stew or soup. Just remember to not overcook them. The use of Sugar Snaps is only limited by your imagination. Many growers say their Sugar Snaps never make it to the kitchen, they are so delicious eaten out of hand, right in the garden.

Ideas for Serving:
"Sugar Snap" peas make an interesting addition to any tossed salad. When making a vegetable gelatin salad, shell the peas and use in the salad. Unmold the salad and surround with the crisp pods filled with any favorite ricotta or cream cheese mixture.

"Sugar Snap" peas can be added to sandwiches. The famous BLT sandwich (bacon, lettuce, tomato) can become BLP (bacon, lettuce, pea).

"Sugar Snaps" make a fabulous substitute for french fries to accompany hamburgers. Just string a handful of snap peas and serve them alongside your hamburger. Try dipping juicy, fresh "Sugar Snaps" into ketchup, mustard and/or mayonnaise.

Casseroles

BROCCOLI AND CHICKEN CASSEROLE

Saute ½ cup chopped onion, ½ cup chopped celery and ¼ cup butter. Add 1 lb. of cooked, drained broccoli to 1 cup cooked rice. Heat 1 can mushroom soup with about 1 cup Cheese Whiz. Heat until cheese is melted. Stir into mixture of celery, onion, broccoli and rice. Add 1½ cups cooked chicken. Put into casserole. Top with slivered almonds. Cover and bake at 350⁰ for 35-45 minutes.

BRUSSELS SPROUTS POLONAISE

2 lbs. brussels sprouts
¼ cup butter
¼ cup fine dry bread crumbs
1 hard-cooked egg yolk, pressed through a fine sieve
2 tablespoons chopped parsley

Wash and trim sprouts and make 2 crosswise cuts in base of each. Cook uncovered in plenty of boiling salted water until just tender, 5-7 minutes. Drain and put in a hot serving dish. Heat butter in a small skillet until it begins to brown. Add bread crumbs and stir until lightly browned. Remove from heat. Add egg yolk and parsley and toss lightly with a fork. Sprinkle over sprouts and toss lightly again. Serve immediately. Serves 6-8.

CARROT TURNIP BAKE

1 large turnip - peeled and cubed
3 large carrots - shredded
2 tablespoons butter
1 egg

2 tablespoons brown sugar
1 cup evaporated milk
1 cup cooked rice

Cook turnip, covered, in boiling water until tender. Drain. Cook carrots until almost tender, drain. Whip turnip, butter, egg, brown sugar, 1 teaspoon salt and dash of pepper until fluffy. Stir in milk, rice and carrots. Turn into baking dish and bake uncovered 35-40 minutes at 350⁰. Serves 12.

TOMATO AND CELERY CASSEROLE

1 - 28 oz. can tomatoes	1 tablespoon flour
2 cups celery - cut in ½ inch pieces	1 tablespoon sugar
1 medium onion - cut fine	1 teaspoon salt

Place vegetables in baking dish. Mix flour, sugar and salt and add to vegetables. Sprinkle 1 cup bread crumbs mixed with 3 tablespoons melted butter, on top of vegetables. Bake one hour at 325°F uncovered.

ITALIAN STYLE ZUCCHINI

¼ cup minced onion	2 cups chopped tomatoes
¼ cup minced green pepper	¼ cup fine, dry bread crumbs
2 tablespoons chopped parsley	¾ cup Italian salad dressing
1 ¼ lb. zucchini - cut into ½ inch pieces	

Combine ingredients in order given, in 2 quart casserole. Cover. Bake in 350°F oven until zucchini is tender, about 1 hour. Stir once during baking. Yields 6 servings.

ZUCCHINI DELUXE

3 large or 6 small zucchini	¼ teaspoon pepper
6 cups fresh bread crumbs	2 tablespoons butter - melted
¼ cup chopped onion	½ lb. process cheese - cubed
1 medium tomato - chopped	¼ cup milk
½ teaspoon salt	6 slices cooked bacon - crumbled

Trim ends of zucchini. Cook, covered, in boiling water (salted) 5-8 minutes, drain. Cut in half lengthwise. Scoop out centre of each, chop. Combine chopped zucchini, bread crumbs, onion, tomato, seasonings, butter; toss lightly. Fill each shell, place in shallow baking dish. Bake at 350°F 25-30 minutes. Heat cheese and milk in saucepan over low heat, stirring until sauce is smooth. Add bacon, serve over zucchini. Makes 6 servings.

LEEK AND POTATO CASSEROLE

4 cups sliced raw potatoes	2 large leeks (1½ cups)
1¾ cups milk	¼ cup fresh bread crumbs
1¼ teaspoon salt	2 tablespoons melted butter

Put potatoes, milk and salt in saucepan. Cover and cook until slightly tender - about 10 minutes. Shake the pan often to prevent potatoes burning. Arrange potatoes and leeks layer by layer in casserole. Combine bread crumbs and butter and sprinkle on top. Bake uncovered for about 20 minutes.

SAUTEED BEEF WITH FRESH VEGETABLES

4 oz. top round or sirloin steak per serving
1 stick celery - cut in ½ inch pieces
½ small green pepper - cut in ½ inch pieces
½ peeled carrot - cut in ½ inch pieces (any fresh vegetables)
¼ head fresh cauliflower - cut in flowerettes
1 fresh broccoli - cut in flowerettes
3 or 4 fresh mushrooms with stems
1 very small piece of fresh garlic and a slice of fresh ginger
cornstarch for thickening
salt and pepper
soya sauce
3-4 green onions for garnish

Marinate the beef with ¼ teaspoon salt, ½ teaspoon sugar, 1 tablespoon soya sauce, 1 teaspoon oil, 1 teaspoon cornstarch and 1 teaspoon brown sugar, for half an hour or longer.

Cook carrots 4-5 minutes, cool in cold water. Boil the rest of the vegetables except mushrooms, green peppers and green onions, for 30-45 seconds. Remove and plunge into cold water and dry them when cold.

Heat the wok, add 2 teaspoons oil. Add garlic, brown and discard. Ginger can be added, browned and discarded. Add beef, saute until 60-65% cooked. Remove.

Put all the vegetables in the wok and fry 2-3 minutes. Add ½-¾ cup water or chicken stock, cover and bring to boil for 2 minutes. Taste and adjust the seasonings and thicken with corn starch. Add beef and mix.

Cut green onions and sprinkle over the dish when cooked.

180

BORSCHT — HOT

1½ cups riced cooked beets
¾ cup stock or water
2 tablespoons onions - grated

3 tablespoons cider vinegar
½ pint sour cream
chopped parsley

Combine beet stock (or water) and onion and heat to boiling. Remove from heat and serve at once with 3 tablespoons of cream and some parsley floating on each serving.

BORSCHT — COLD

1½ lbs. beets, peeled and chopped
1 medium onion, chopped
juice of 2 lemons, rind of one
    lemon
2 cups water

4 cups milk
3 eggs
3 egg yolks
3 teaspoons sugar
Worcestershire sauce

Boil the beets and onions in water until cooked. Simmer grated lemon rind and juice in a little water for a few minutes and strain into beets. Heat milk. Beat eggs and carefully add to the milk, stirring constantly. Do not boil. Add dash of Worcestershire sauce, sugar, salt and pepper to taste, to the egg mixture. Strain and combine with the beets. Chill and serve very cold with a tablespoon of sour cream on each serving.

ZUCCHINI LASAGNE

1 lb. ground beef
1 clove garlic - crushed
1 tablespoon chopped parsley
1 tablespoon basil
1 teaspoon salt
2 cups cooked tomatoes
2 - 6 oz. cans tomato paste
2 medium zucchini

3 cups cream-style cottage cheese
2 beaten eggs
¼ teaspoon salt
½ teaspoon pepper
2 tablespoons chopped parsley
½ cup grated Parmesan cheese
1 lb. Mozzarella cheese - sliced
    thin

Brown meat slowly; spoon off excess fat. Add next 6 ingredients to meat. Simmer, uncovered, till thick - about 30 minutes, stirring occasionally. Combine the cottage cheese with the eggs, salt, pepper, parsley and Parmesan cheese. Slice a layer of zucchini in the bottom of a 13 x 9 x 2 baking dish; spread cottage cheese mixture over. Add half the Mozzarella cheese and half the meat mixture. Repeat layers. Bake in moderate oven (375°F) for 30 minutes. Let stand 10-15 minutes before cutting in squares. Makes 12 servings. Hint - A layer of chopped spinach may be added as well.

Desserts
Cakes ★ Cookies ★ Pies ★ Quick Breads

BEET AND CARROT LOAF CAKE

Beat together:

¾ cup salad oil
1½ cups sugar
3 egg yolks

1 teaspoon vanilla
3 tablespoons hot water

Add sifted:

2 cups flour
3 teaspoons baking powder

¼ teaspoon salt
1 teaspoon cinnamon

Then add:

1 cup grated raw beets
1 cup grated raw carrots
½ cup coconut or walnuts or raisins

Fold in beaten egg whites, pour into greased angel cake pan or 2 loaf pans. Bake at 350⁰F oven, 50-60 minutes, or in loaf pans from 30-40 minutes. (I like to put wax paper in bottom of pan).

CARROT CAKE WITH PINEAPPLE

Sift together:

2 cups all purpose flour
2 teaspoons baking powder
½ teaspoon baking soda

2 teaspoons cinnamon
1 teaspoon salt

Beat 4 eggs. Gradually add 1½ cups white sugar, beat until light and fluffy. Add 1 cup cooking oil, blend. Add flour mixture. Add 2 cups grated carrots and 1 can (14 oz.) crushed pineapple (drained). Bake in 3 layers or in large 14"x11"x2" pan at 350⁰F for 30-35 minutes for layers and 50-60 minutes for large pan.

Frosting: Mix butter, icing sugar and pineapple juice to make icing.

CARROT COOKIES

½ cup soft butter
1½ cup brown sugar
2 eggs
2 cups sifted all purpose flour
2 teaspoons baking powder
½ teaspoon soda

½ teaspoon salt
1 teaspoon nutmeg
2 cups quick cooking rolled oats
1 cup finely grated raw carrot
1 cup chopped dates

Heat oven to 350°F. Grease cookie sheet. Beat butter, sugar and eggs together until fluffy. Sift flour, baking powder, soda, salt and nutmeg together into first mixture and stir to blend. Stir in rolled oats, dates and carrots. Drop by teaspoons onto prepared cookie sheets. Flatten slightly with fork and bake 12-15 minutes or until set and nicely browned.

CHOCOLATE-ZUCCHINI CAKE

2½ cups whole-wheat flour
½ cup toasted wheat germ
½ cup carob (cocoa)
2½ teaspoons baking powder
1½ teaspoons baking soda
1 teaspoon each salt and cinnamon
¾ cup butter or margarine - softened
1 cup packed brown sugar
1 cup granulated sugar
3 eggs
2 teaspoons vanilla
2 teaspoons grated lemon peel
2 cups coarsely grated, unpeeled zucchini (2 large)
½ cup milk
1 cup chopped walnuts
1 cup raisins
Lemon glaze (recipe follows)

Stir together flour, wheat germ, cocoa, baking powder, soda, salt and cinnamon; set aside. In large bowl of mixer, cream butter and sugars. Add eggs and beat until fluffy. With spoon, stir in vanilla, lemon peel and zucchini until well blended. Stir in milk alternately with flour mixture. Stir in walnuts and raisins. Turn into floured, greased 3-quart fluted or plain tube pan (10 inch). Bake in preheated 375°F oven 45 minutes or until pick inserted in centre comes out clean. Cool in pan 10 minutes then turn out on rack to cool completely. Drizzle with lemon glaze (see p. 184). Makes 12-16 servings.

Lemon Glaze: Beat 2 cups confectioners' sugar, 1 teaspoon grated lemon peel (optional) and 3 tablespoons lemon juice until smooth. If too thick to drizzle, thin with a little more juice.

CARROT PIE

2 cups pureed cooked carrot	½ cup brown sugar
2 eggs	½ teaspoon nutmeg
1 cup milk	½ teaspoon cinnamon
¼ cup butter	⅛ teaspoon ginger

Pour into unbaked pie shell. Oven heat 375°F. Bake 45-50 minutes.

CRABAPPLE PIE

Line 9" pie plate with pie crust and sprinkle with 10 broken soda crackers. Beat together 1 cup sugar, 1 cup crabapple pulp (left over from making jelly), 1¼ cups water and ½ teaspoon cream of tartar. Pour into pie plate, dot with 1 tablespoon butter, sprinkle with cinnamon and cover with top crust. Bake in 450°F oven for 10 minutes, then reduce heat to 350°F for 20-25 minutes until golden brown. Serve with hot custard poured over top.

PINEAPPLE ZUCCHINI LOAF

3 eggs
1 cup oil
1¾ cups crushed pineapple (well drained)
3 cups flour
1 teaspoon soda
1½ teaspoons cinnamon
1 cup chopped nuts
1¾ cups sugar
1¾ cups grated, unpeeled zucchini
2 teaspoons vanilla
1 teaspoon salt
¼ teaspoon baking powder
¾ teaspoon nutmeg

Beat eggs until light and fluffy, add sugar and beat till blended. Stir in oil, vanilla, zucchini and pineapple. Sift dry ingredients, stir into egg mixture along with nuts. Turn into 2 greased and floured loaf pans. Bake at 350°F for 50-60 minutes.

RHUBARB CAKE

2 cups sugar
½ cup shortening
1 egg - beaten
1 teaspoon baking soda
2 cups flour
1 teaspoon salt

1 cup sour milk
2 cups chopped rhubarb - floured
1 teaspoon vanilla
½ teaspoon cinnamon and
    ¼ cup butter

Cream shortening and 1½ cups sugar. Add egg and beat well. Sift together flour, soda and salt. Add alternately with milk or creamed mixture. Add rhubarb and vanilla, mix well. Pour into 9"x13" pan. Mix cinnamon, butter and remaining sugar until crumbly. Sprinkle over batter. Bake at 350°F for 45 minutes.

SASKATOON PIE

1 - 9" pie shell - uncooked, and
    top for same
3 cups fresh or frozen saskatoons
1½ cups cold water

½ cup sugar
2 tablespoons corn starch
1 tablespoon lemon juice or
    more if needed

Put saskatoons into saucepan with cold water and cook until tender. The secret of cooking saskatoons is NOT to add sugar until they are cooked. Then add sugar, lemon juice and cornstarch dissolved in a little cold water. Cook until thick. If desired, put a layer of raspberries (fresh or frozen) or rhubarb or gooseberries or tart apple slices in the pie shell. Then pour saskatoon sauce over and put the top on, sealing the edges with water. Bake at 375°F until nicely browned. It may need more sugar if you add the layer of fruit in the bottom. Also, sprinkle the raw fruit layer with a little Minute Tapioca to absorb the extra juice.

STRAWBERRY OR RASPBERRY SHORT CAKE

Save a few whole berries for decoration.
Slice or crush 1½-2 cups fresh fruit and sugar to taste.
Cake: 1 cup flour
       2 teaspoons baking powder
       1 tablespoon sugar

1 small egg
2 tablespoons corn oil
½ cup milk

Sift dry ingredients together in a bowl. Beat together egg, oil and milk and add to sifted dry ingredients. Mix lightly. Bake in greased 8" round pan 15-20 minutes at 400°F. Cool but don't allow to get cold. Turn out on plate. Split in half. Put half of the fruit on bottom half. Cover with whipped cream. Put other half of cake on top and cover with remaining fruit. Top with whipping cream and decorate with whole berries.

Beverages

BLACK CURRANT ICE

1½ cups black currants
1 cup granulated sugar
1 tablespoon lemon juice

⅛ teaspoon salt
3 egg whites

Place currants and 1 cup water in a saucepan. Cover and bring to a boil. Reduce heat to low and simmer for 15 minutes or until mushy. Press through sieve and discard seeds and skins.

Meanwhile, combine sugar with 1 cup water and boil for 5 minutes. Cool and combine with black currant juice (puree), lemon juice and salt. Pour into shallow cake pan.

When the outside is frozen (but inside still mushy) put into blender and blend until the ice crystals are broken down. Do not let mixture melt. Beat egg whites until stiff and fold gently into the semi frozen puree.

Pack into containers, cover and freeze. Let soften in refrigerator about 20 minutes before serving.

RASPBERRY MINT DRINK

Combine 1 cup sugar, 1 cup water and the grated rind of 2 lemons. Cook, stirring over low heat until sugar is dissolved. Boil 5 minutes. Cool. Add 2 cups crushed raspberries, 1 cup lemon juice and 4 more cups of water. Serve in glass garnished with mint leaves.

ROSY RHUBARB PUNCH

2 lbs. (7-8 cups) rhubarb
3 cups water
1 - 6 oz. can frozen pink lemonade

2 - 6 oz. cans water
½ cup sugar
1 large bottle ginger ale

Add 3 cups water to rhubarb. Simmer until tender. Strain, chill juice, (there will be approximately 4 cups juice). To the chilled juice add frozen lemonade, 2 cans water and sugar. Add ginger ale just before serving.

RHUBARB OR CRABAPPLE JUICE

Wash and chop fruit. Fill large container with fruit (glass, plastic, pottery but *not aluminum*).

Cover with boiling water and let stand 12 to 24 hours. Pour juice off. Add ½ cup sweetener, preferably honey to each quart of juice. Heat to 180°F. Pour into hot sterilized jars and seal. Juice jars with rubber lined lids are ideal jars for this purpose. When ready to use, add 1½ times as much water. Rhubarb added to any other juice will take on the flavour of that juice.

Jams ★ Jellies ★ Marmalades
Conserves ★ Syrups

CARROT MARMALADE

15 cups carrots (blender "chop")   7 oranges - chopped
12 cups sugar   1 large tin crushed pineapple
7 lemons - chopped

Let stand overnight. Re-blend at "grind". Boil briskly for 15 minutes.
Seal hot in sterilized jars.

CHOKECHERRY JELLY

Chokecherries contain little or no pectin, so in order to make them jell,
the use of pectin rich crabapples or pectin is essential. If jelly does not
jell, it still makes delicious pancake syrup or base for cool summer drink.

4 cups chokecherry juice   8 cups sugar
4 cups crabapple juice   1 bottle pectin

To prepare juice: wash and clean about 1 gallon pail of berries. Add 4
cups water and boil until tender. Put in jelly bag and drain juice off. Do
same with crabapples.

Measure 2 cups each of chokecherry juice and crabapple juice into large,
heavy saucepan. Bring to boil and add 4 cups sugar, stirring to dissolve
sugar. Bring to full rolling boil and add ½ bottle pectin. Boil hard for 1
minute. Test for jelling. Using a shiny spoon, dip in the jelly and let it run
off spoon. When drops thicken along edge of spoon and run together
before falling off, jelly is ready. Remove from heat. Stir and skim. Pour
into hot, sterilized jelly glasses and cover with wax immediately. Repeat
with other batch. It is best not to try making too big a batch at one time.
Smaller quantities seem to jell best.

CHOKECHERRY SYRUP

9 cups chokecherries
2½ cups water

Boil, covered, 15 minutes. Place in jelly bag, squeeze out juice. Yields 4
cups juice. Put juice in large pan, add 8½ cups sugar. Boil 1 minute.
Pour in sterilized jars and seal. Very good on pancakes.

CRABAPPLE JELLY

Cover apples with water just until they float. Boil 20 minutes or until they are cooked down. Put in cheese cloth to drip overnight. Measure out 10 cups of juice and 10 cups sugar. Put in large kettle and bring to boil. Boil until it foams up once (about 25 minutes). Skim off foam and pour into clean jars. Seal with wax.

CRABAPPLE AND ROWAN JELLY

Equal weight of crab apples and Rowans (Mountain Ash berries).

Method: Cut crabapples into pieces and Rowans off the stem. Put in kettle with enough water, just showing through the fruit. Boil till soft. Pour into jelly bag. When strained, add cup for cup of granulated sugar. Boil till jellying stage. Test frequently as Rowans are rich in pectin. Pour into sterilized jars and seal.

FIG AND RHUBARB JAM

Cut any amount of rhubarb into small pieces and let stand 12-15 hours in half the amount of sugar. Boil till thick. Add cooked figs cut in small pieces and return to boil. Pour into jars and seal.

GREEN TOMATO MINCEMEAT

3 quarts finely chopped green tomatoes. (Cover with water and boil 1 hour. Let stand overnight and drain).

Salt	½ lb. suet
1 quart finely chopped apples	1 cup vinegar
2½ lbs. brown sugar	1 teaspoon cinnamon
½ lb. mixed peel	1 teaspoon cloves
1 lb. raisins	1 teaspoon nutmeg
½ lb. currants	

Bring above ingredients to boil. Bottle and seal hot.

QUICK RASPBERRY JAM

Use fairly large, heavy pan. To each heaping cup of raspberries, allow ¾ cup sugar. Put fruit and half sugar in pan. Bring to boil, being careful not to let it stick. Add remaining sugar. Bring to full rolling boil and time 1½ minutes, stirring gently. Take off fire and put in sterilized jars. This method retains fresh fruit color and flavor.

MINT JELLY

1 cup fresh mint leaves
¼ cup boiling water

2¾ cups sugar
1 quart crapapple juice

Wash mint leaves, snip from stems, add boiling water and 2½ cups sugar. Let stand a few hours. Bring to boiling point, strain through several layers of cheesecloth. Add remaining ¼ cup sugar to apple juice, stir until it reacts to jelly test. Skim and pour into hot sterilized jelly glasses. Seal with paraffin.

RHUBARB CONSERVE

14 cups rhubarb
3 cups raisins
7 cups sugar

juice of 2 oranges
rind of 2 oranges - thinly sliced

Combine and let stand ½ hour. Bring to boil, boil uncovered for 40 minutes, stirring frequently. Add ½-1 cup chopped walnuts and boil to jam stage, about 5 minutes. Pour into hot, sterilized jars. Cool and seal. Yields 12 cups.

SASKATOON JELLY

3 cups berry juice
7½ cups sugar

½ cup lemon juice
1 bottle liquid pectin

To prepare fruit: clean ripened berries (about 4 lbs.). Place in kettle and crush. Heat gently until juice starts to flow, then simmer covered 15 minutes. Place in jelly cloth and squeeze out juice. Squeeze and strain juice from 4 lemons.

To make jelly: Measure sugar and juice into large saucepan and mix. Add lemon juice and combine well. Bring to boil over high heat and at once add pectin, stirring constantly. Then bring to full rolling boil and boil hard for 1 minute. Remove from heat, skim, pour quickly into jars, seal with wax.

SASKATOON AND RHUBARB JAM

1 quart saskatoons
1 quart rhubarb

3 cups sugar

Cut rhubarb in small pieces and put in covered saucepan with saskatoons and a little water. Bring mixture to boil. Cook until desired thickness. Add sugar and bring to boil. Pour into jars and seal.

ZUCCHINI BUTTER

4 lbs. zucchini or vegetable marrow. Steam until tender. Drain well and add ½ lb. butter, 4 lbs. sugar, 6 lemons (rind and juice). Mash. Simmer 10 minutes or until a smooth paste. Add preserved ginger if you like it that way.

ZUCCHINI MARMALADE

A good way to use up over sized zucchini.
Peel and remove seeds. Chop and measure:

> 6 cups zucchini
> 6 cups sugar
> 1 large orange
> 1 lemon - ground

Let stand overnight. Bring to boil. Simmer for 1 hour. Seal in jars.

Sauces ★ Pickles
Chutneys ★ Etc.

BREAD AND BUTTER PICKLES

6 quarts cucumbers
2 red peppers
½ cup salt
3 cups sugar
3 teaspoons tumeric

3 teaspoons celery seed
12 medium onions
6 cups vinegar
whole cloves
2 tablespoons mustard seed

Cook together until cucumbers appear clear. Bottle hot.

CHILI SAUCE

7½ lbs. ripe tomatoes - peeled and chopped

Grind in food chopper:
6 medium onions (2½ cups)
6 red and green peppers - mixed (2½ cups)
3 cups celery - finely shredded or chopped

Put in large kettle and add:
3 cups sugar
2 tablespoons salt
4 cups cider vinegar

1½ sticks cinnamon
1 tablespoon garlic salt

In cheese cloth bag put:
1 tablespoon whole cloves
3 tablespoons whole allspice

Drop the bag in mixture and cook for 2½-3 hours. Makes about 8 pints. This sauce has a superb flavor. Put in hot jars and seal.

GREEN TOMATO PICKLES (SWEET)

8 lbs. peeled tomatoes, sprinkle with ½ cup salt, let stand overnight, drain.

6 cups sugar
1 quart vinegar

½ oz. whole cloves
6 sticks cinnamon

Boil tomatoes in this til tender. Let stand 2 days. Drain. Boil juice and pour over tomatoes. Repeat twice from "let stand". Put tomatoes in jars. Boil juice and seal hot.

HORSE RADISH

Dig roots in late fall or early spring (months with "R" in them). Peel under water. Cut in short lengths. Grind (outside in open air). Add 2 cups white sugar and enough white vinegar to cover; enough for 1 gallon of ground horseradish mix. Place in sterilized jars, leaving head room and freeze. To serve, add more vinegar and sugar if it seems dry. Great with roast beef. In hard times, use with cottage cheese.

MINT SAUCE

Prepare 4 cups of ground mint leaves. Use only the mint leaves, not the stems. Wash and dry mint leaves. Put through fine screen on food chopper. Boil 2 cups sugar in 1 quart vinegar for 1 minute. Add mint leaves and simmer for 10 minutes. Pour into jars and seal. Goes well with lamb.

PICKLED BEETS

Cook beets until tender, peel. Cut in desired pieces. Heat enough vinegar to cover beets, using 1 cup sugar to 1 cup vinegar, salt to taste. When vinegar mixture is boiling, add cut-up beets and bring to boiling point again. Put into sterilized jars and seal. If desired, a few whole cloves and allspice may be added to each jar. These may be drained, butter added, heated and served as a vegetable.

PICKLED CARROTS (Quart Size)

1 quart small carrots	1 cup sugar
½ cup water	3 tablespoons pickling spice
3 cups white vinegar	

Cook carrots until skins slip easily and carrots half done. Slip off skins. Boil together 10 minutes the vinegar, water, sugar and spice. Remove spice. Add carrots and boil 2-4 minutes or until tender. Pack in hot, sterile jars, pour syrup over and seal.

Variations: Pickled shoestring carrots for cocktail.
Cut carrots after parboiling, into uniform strips. Follow the above directions but do not boil the sticks in syrup. Barely bring them to boiling point. Pack and seal.

THOUSAND ISLE PICKLE

8 cucumbers
12 large onions

1 large cauliflower
2 red and 2 green peppers

Sauce:

8 cups mild vinegar
6 cups sugar
1 tablespoon mustard seed
1 tablespoon celery seed

¾ cup flour
1 tablespoon dry mustard
1 tablespoon tumeric

Method: Chop vegetables - soak 1 hour in ½ cup salt, 5 cups water, strain. Put vegetables in sauce and boil 20 minutes. Bottle.

ZUCCHINI PICKLES

2 lbs. small zucchini
2 medium onions
¼ cup pure granulated sugar
1 pint white vinegar
1 cup sugar

1 teaspoon celery seed
1 teaspoon mustard seed
1 teaspoon tumeric
½ teaspoon dry mustard

Wash and cut unpeeled zucchini and peeled onion in very thin slices into crock or bowl. Cover with water, add salt. Let stand 1 hour. Drain. Mix remaining ingredients and bring to boil. Pour over zucchini-onion mixture. Let stand 1 hour. Bring to boil and cook 3 minutes. Pack in hot, sterilized jars to within ½ inch of top and seal. Yields 3 pints.

HAMBURGER RELISH

12 large ripe tomatoes
12 large apples - chopped
9 medium onions - chopped
2 cups sugar
1 pint white vinegar
1 teaspoon pepper

½ teaspoon celery salt
½ teaspoon cloves
½ teaspoon allspice
1 teaspoon cinnamon
¼ cup salt

Blend all ingredients. Cook until thick. Pour while hot into sterilized jars. Seal.

ZUCCHINI RELISH

Good way to use up over-sized zucchini. Peel and grind 10 cups zucchini. Grind 1 cup onion. Add 5 tablespoons salt. Mix together and let stand overnight. In morning, drain and rinse with cold water. Add:

2¼ cups vinegar	1 teaspoon mustard seed
4-6 cups sugar	½ teaspoon pepper
1 teaspoon celery seed	1 chopped red pepper (large)

Mix all and cook 30 minutes - longer if too watery. Seal. Makes 8 pints.

RIPE TOMATO CHUTNEY

14 medium size ripe tomatoes - peeled
7 apples - peeled and cut in pieces
7 medium onions - chopped
2 cups vinegar
¾ lb. brown sugar
¼ cup white sugar
½ lb. raisins
¾ teaspoon each - cloves, allspice, ginger and cinnamon
1 tablespoon salt - may need a little more.

Boil all together until thick. Pour into sterilized jars and seal. Makes about 7 pints.

SPICED CRABAPPLES

Select good flavored, rosy-cheeked crabapples. Wash well, leaving stems on. Remove the blossom ends and prick with needle several times.

6 lbs. crabapples	6 cups sugar (or less)
3 cups vinegar	1 teaspoon whole cloves
3 cups water or beet water from cooking beets.	1 three inch stick cinnamon

Put vinegar, water, sugar and spices (tied in bag) in kettle and boil for 5 minutes. Add crabapples and simmer gently till tender, but do not overcook. Pack in sterilized jars, cover with boiling syrup and seal.

Another Method: Pack raw apples into hot jars, cover with boiling syrup and process in hot water bath for 20 minutes. These are delicious served with pork, chicken or ham.

 **Helpful Hints**

Put a piece of horseradish in dill pickles for added zip and flavour.

Miscellaneous

TOASTED SUNFLOWER SEEDS

Cut heads off sunflowers when seeds start to turn brown. Hang heads upside down in warm place to dry. Remove seeds and soak overnight in salt water. Dry and then roast in 200°F oven for 3 hours or until crisp. Sunflower seeds are very nutritious.

TOASTED PUMPKIN SEEDS

#1   Don't throw away those wet, string-laden seeds from your pumpkin. They are a delicious treat! Wash seeds and remove strings to the best of ability. Let seeds soak in salted water overnight. (½ teaspoons salt per ⅔ cup water). Then place seeds in low baking pan in oven at 300°F for approximately 20 minutes or till golden. Eat with or without removing shells. Any squash seeds can be prepared in same way, but not as tasty as pumpkin.

#2   Spread pumpkin seeds over baking sheet. Bake in 375°F oven for 30 minutes until seeds dry and fluff up slightly. Stir frequently. Cool. Store in airtight container. Before eating, sprinkle with salt, if desired.

#3   Wash fresh pumpkin seeds in bowl using warm water to remove fibers. Drain and blot dry. Coat seeds with melted butter and spread them out on cookie sheet. Sprinkle seed to taste with salt. Place in slow oven 250°F for 20-30 minutes until they are light golden in color.

BABY FOOD

Puree *cooked* vegetables in blender using cooling liquid to bring to very smooth consistency. Do not add salt, sugar or butter. Carrots, peas, wax beans, green beans and yellow squash are recommended vegetables for babies. Place puree in ice cube containers. NOTE: If you don't have a blender, prepare pureed home grown vegetables for baby by using a strainer, a sieve or grinder, and freeze. When frozen, empty cubes into freezer bag, label, date and use as needed. To serve, place frozen or thawed cube in a cup, place in a saucepan with ½ inch water and heat.

Washed berries, i.e. blueberries, saskatoons, may be pressed through strainer or food mill to remove skins and seeds and frozen in ice cube trays. One quart berries yields approximately 2 cups puree or 10 food cubes. Do not add sweetening. Berries such as raspberries and strawberries contain a great many seeds - if you cannot remove the seeds then avoid using these berries. Do not use cranberries.

For more information on preparing baby foods from your home grown fruits and vegetables, contact your local health clinic or District Home Economist.

ROSE HIPS

There is more than just beauty in a wild rose. The little berry that follows the blossoms and gives added beauty to our fall foliage has health value too. It is one of the richest known sources of vitamin C. Three average rose hips contain as much vitamin C as one medium sized orange. Rose hips have some property which prevents loss of vitamin C during cooking, canning or drying.

Collecting Rose Hips

The ripe hips that are vivid red and slightly soft are best, although green hips are also rich in vitamin C. Hips that are green or semi-ripe have more pectin and are better for jelly and jam than ripe hips. Some prefer the flavor of the hips when picked after the first frost. There is a gradual loss of vitamin C and a tendency to mould if there is a lengthy delay between picking and bottling the rose hips, therefore, preserve as soon as possible.

Ways to use Rose Hips

Once you have tried rose hips you will find that there are many ways to use them in foods served on the daily menu.

#1. Rose hips puree or syrup, fresh or canned can be used in baked products such as bread, buns, biscuits, drop cookies, cake, gingerbread. Add ¼ cup of puree to recipe. It may be necessary to reduce the liquid a little except in muffins. If using juice or syrup, use about 2 tablespoons or more to replace equal amount of liquid in recipe. The flavor will not be noticed in foods with distinct flavors such as spice or molasses, but not so suitable for more delicate flavored cakes or cookies.

#2. Rose hip puree can be added to desserts such as ice cream, or fruit whip. Up to 6-8 tablespoons can be added to a batch of ice cream without the flavor being discerned.

#3. Rose hip puree or syrup can be added to soups. Try adding 1-2 tablespoons to potato or vegetable soup.

#4. To make an excellent spread for toast, muffins or hot cakes, combine: 1 part rose hip puree to 3 parts honey.

#5. Simply pick raw hips and eat or serve seeded and chopped or cut in halves, in salads or sandwich fillings. Be sure to remove seeds and most of the hairs as they are irritating to the digestive tract.

#6. Rose hip puree can be used in sandwich fillings combined with cheese, canned salmon, peanut butter, etc.

RECIPES

Canned Rose Hip Puree

Wash hips, remove stems and hull. Put through food chopper using medium knife. Cover completely with water and simmer until quite tender (about 5 minutes). Press through sieve. Can without sugar by processing in pint sealers for 30 minutes or add ½ cup sugar or honey to each cup of puree. Boil 5 minutes and bottle in sterilized jars.

Rose Hip Syrup

Wash hips, remove stems and hull. Put through food chopper using medium knife. Cover completely with 3 pints boiling water to 2 lbs. hips and boil for 2 minutes. Using sieve, run as much liquid through as can be put through without effort. Drain remainder using jelly bag or 2 thicknesses of fine cheese cloth. Measure liquid (should be 1½ pints), if more, boil down. This juice may be bottled and processed for 15 minutes without sugar, although upon opening, it does not keep as long as with sugar. To make syrup: Add ¾ cup sugar (or less), boil 5 minutes. Bottle in hot sterilized sealers or small bottles and process 10 minutes. Using small bottles, such as vanilla that do not seal, dip top of bottle in paraffin wax immediately upon removing from water bath.

Canned Whole Rose Hips

Wash hips, stem and hull. To save time during the busy canning season, these may be canned whole. Pack in sealer to within ½ inch of top, cover with hot water and process for 30 minutes. To use later: Press through sieve and strain through cheese cloth. Use as puree or just drain in jelly bag and use as juice or syrup.

Dried Rose Hips

Cut in halves, lengthwise and dry in warm oven, turning occasionally. Be careful not to overheat or they will turn brown in color. When properly dried they are a distinct red color. They can also be dried in a food dehydrator. When dry, remove hairs and seeds by shaking in a corn popper or two sieves tied together. A fan helps to blow out hairs. Store in covered jars in a dry place. To use, soak and boil in water until consistency of puree or tomato sauce. Use as puree. The dried hips can also be used to make a tea.

Rose Hip and Fruit Jelly

Use rose hips that are green or semi-ripe, as ripe hips have very little pectin. A better jelly is obtained if commercial pectin is used. A batch of jelly will take about ½ package crystal pectin. Jellies made with all or part honey seem to have a better flavor. A little acid, such as lemon juice, adds to the flavor. Most rose hip products will be softer at first but will stiffen on standing. Do not place in sun to stiffen as this destroys vitamin C.

A.   Rose Hip and Crabapple Jelly

Use ½ crabapple juice and ½ rose hip puree. To 1 cup of this mixture, use ¾ cup sugar or honey. Less rose puree may be used, e.g., 1 part puree to 3 parts crabapple if flavour of rose hip is not desired.

B.   Rose Hip and Other Fruit Jelly and Jam

Rose hip puree may be combined in jelly and jam without fruit such as cranberry, grape, chokecherry, red currant, etc. Combine 1 part rose hip puree to 2 parts fruit or ⅓ if rose hip flavor is not desired. Honey and lemon add to flavor.

Rose Hip Catsup

4 quarts ripe rose hips	1 clove garlic
2 medium size onions	1 cup water (more if necessary)

Boil these ingredients until they are soft. Strain. Add ¾ cup brown sugar. Tie in bag and add:

½ tablespoon whole allspice	½ tablespoon celery seed
½ tablespoon whole mace	2 inch stick cinnamon
½ tablespoon whole cloves	

Boil these ingredients quickly. Add: 1 cup vinegar, cayenne and salt if desired. Boil catsup 10 minutes longer. Bottle at once in sterilized jars or bottles. Seal bottles with wax. The flavor of the catsup is excellent.

Rose Hip and Apple Juice Cocktail

1 tablespoon rose hip puree
1 teaspoon honey
2 cups apple juice

Mix rose hip puree and honey. Stir mixture into chilled apple juice.

ABC Sandwich Filling

1 tablespoon honey	1 small carrot - grated
1 teaspoon rose hip puree	

Sufficient wheat germ to thicken the mixture to sandwich spread consistency.

This is a very nutritious sandwich, the carrots provide vitamin A, the wheat germ, B vitamins and the rose hip puree, vitamin C. The honey adds energy and makes it taste good. It is particularly good on rye or whole wheat bread.

FOOD DRYING
by Dorothy Jackson

"Waste not, want not," is as true today as when the axiom was coined years ago. Drying is the oldest method of food preservation known to man, and is still the most economical. Add to the fun, cut the cost, increase the variety with food gems you prepare yourself.

You don't have to have a food dryer or take a special course to learn about food drying; these tools help but several dried foods can be prepared at home with only a little basic knowledge and no special equipment. Once you try food drying, however, you'll probably enjoy it so much that you'll want to go further into this old time art!

Dried foods have several advantages:
- they're compact
- they're light weight
- they keep several seasons
- they're healthful: more food value is preserved than by methods using higher heat or water, there are no additives or chemicals
- they taste good
- they're versatile
- they cost little or are even free

What Can you Dry? — Almost anything! Fruits, fruit leathers, vegetables, meats, poultry (as jerky), nuts and herbs. There are several excellent books on food drying and information is also available from your local District Home Economist. The reference book that I have found most useful is *Dry and Save* by Dora D. Flack. It is considered a complete guide to food drying at home including many recipes. Another good book published by H.P. Books with lots of colored illustrations and information is *Drying Foods*.

The drying of foods has opened up an exciting and interesting new way of food preparation and eating in our home. The possibilities for the use of dried foods is endless. I'm sure if you dry it — you'll like it!

Fruit Leather: *Dorothy Jackson*

Fruit leathers are fruit purees dried to a nonsticky, pliable texture. They are sold in health food stores but you can make your own at a fraction of the cost and yours will not contain perservatives. Leathers can be made from single fruits or combinations of two or more, sweetened with honey if you like, made tart with lemon, or flavoured with spices.

200

Basic Instructions:
1. Use very ripe fruit.
2. Use a blender to reduce fruit to a pulp. Add only enough liquid to blend. (Some fruits blend better if cooked a little first: apples, rhubarb, peaches).
3. When puree is smooth add desired sweetening. Ripe sweet fruit requires nothing more.
4. Line a cookie sheet with plastic wrap. Anchor wrap with tape at corners to prevent wrap from flopping over puree.
5. Pour puree over plastic and smooth out.
6. Put in dehydrator or you can use the oven with the setting on low 150°-200°F, leave the oven door open about one inch.
7. Most leathers will dry in 6 to 12 hours although I've had some take up to 24 hours to dry. It depends on the kind of fruit, its thickness and humidity.
8. When leather can be pulled completely free of plastic it is dried. Don't overdry; it should be chewy but not stiff.
9. Store rolled in plastic wrap or store in tall glass jars.
10. Tear off a piece and start chewing or make into pinwheels.

Leather Pinwheels:
Spread filling over a sheet of leather. Roll like a cinnamon roll and slice like salami.

   ½ cup liquid honey
   1 cup non-instant dry milk
   1 tblsp. butter
   ½ tsp. vanilla
   ½ to 1 cup coconut
   ½ cup chopped nuts (optional - can use peanuts, chashews, seasame seeds)
   ½ cup ground apples or pears (optional)

Stir, then knead honey, dry milk, butter, vanilla together. Add remaining ingredients and spread on a sheet of fruit leather. Roll, chill, and slice with a very sharp knife. If there is any left after serving, store in freezer.

Index

207

Sweet William, 78
Swiss Chard, 79, **126**

Tagetes, 6, 7, 71, 75, 76, 79, 104
Tamarack, **50**
Thalictrum, 88
Thyme, 16, 68, 109, **129**
Tickseed, 75, 76
Tidy Tips, 75
Tiger Flowers, 104
Tomatoes, 5, 7, 19, **21**, 71, 76, 80, 104,
   126, 137, 138
Tomato Cold Frame, 21
Trace Elements, 14
Transplanting, 6, 7, **38**
   plants, 6, 7
   shrubs, 34, **38**
   trees, 34, **38**
   wild, large deciduous trees, **38**
   wild, large evergreen trees, **38**
Trees, **33**, 155
   fertilizing, **35**
   for birds, 38, **141**
   for colour, 37
   for foundation planting, 38
   for hedges, 38
   native 45, 65
   planting, **34**, **37**
   propagation from cuttings, **60**
   propagation from seeds, **59**
   pruning, **36**, 39
   spacing, 29
   transplanting wild, **38**
   watering, 35
   winter care, **34**, **57**
Trollius, 84, 90
Tropaeolum, 75, 104
Tulips 82, 83, 91, 92
Turnip, 7, **127**
Turnip Maggot, 18

Vegetables, **119**, 137
Vegetable Garden Rotation, 120
Vegetable Companion Planting, **19**
Verbena, 75, 80, 111

Veronica, 90, 111
Vermiculite, 72, 93
Viability of seeds, 78
Viburnum trilobum, 30, 37, 38, 143, 146
Vinca minor, 68
Vines, 38
Viola, 78, 109
Violets, 100
Virginia Creeper, 38, 68
Viscaria, 75

Water and Watering, 84, 92, 103, 104,
   108, **120**, 133
Weed Control, 14, 146
Weeping Birch, 50
Western Sandcherry, 37
White Birch, **50**
White Spruce, **44**
Wild Geranium, 49
Wild Gooseberry, 46
Wild Strawberry, 49
Willow
   Laurel Leaf, 30, 37, 61
   Pussy, 30, 61
   Silver, 46
Wild Blue Flax, 88
Wild Flowers in the Garden, 100
Wind Breaks, **61**
Window Boxes and Planters, 105
   choice of plants, 105
   soil mix, 105
   types of containers, 105
Winter Care, 35, 54, 85
Wintergreen, 30, **48**
Wolf Willow, 37, 46
Wood Ashes, 13, 16, 17, 18, 87

Xeranthemum, **113**

Yard Planning, **23**

Zinnia, 6, 7
Zucchini, **126**

Order a Copy for a Friend!

Millarville Horticultural Club
Box 76
Millarville, Alberta
T0L 1K0
(403) 931-3119
(403) 256-9100

Name _____

Address _____

Province _____ Postal Code _____

Please send _____ copies of "Gardening Under The Arch" at $13.00 each, plus $3.00 each for postage and handling.

Total amount enclosed $_____

Make cheque or money order payable to "Millarville Horticultural Club". Price subject to change after December 31, 1995.

— —

Order a Copy for a Friend!

Millarville Horticultural Club
Box 76
Millarville, Alberta
T0L 1K0
(403) 931-3119
(403) 256-9100

Name _____

Address _____

Province _____ Postal Code _____

Please send _____ copies of "Gardening Under The Arch" at $13.00 each, plus $3.00 each for postage and handling.

Total amount enclosed $_____

Make cheque or money order payable to "Millarville Horticultural Club". Price subject to change after December 31, 1995.